how to start a home-based

Makeup Artist Business

d.d. Nickel

Guilford, Connecticut

Copyright © 2012 by Morris Book Publishing, LLC

Spot art licensed by shutterstock.com

Editorial Director: Cynthia Hughes Cullen
Editor: Tracee Williams
Project Editor: Lauren Brancato
Text Design: Sheryl P. Kober
Layout: Sue Murray

ISSN 2166-353X
ISBN 978-0-7627-7863-8

Printed in the United States of America
10 9 8 7 6 5 4 3 2 1

Dedicated to my parents, Donald and Barbara Nickel, for not only encouraging and supporting my creativity, but for giving me the freedom to be myself.

Contents

Contents   vii

Acknowledgments

Many thanks to Tracee Williams and Globe Pequot Press for giving me the opportunity to share everything I know about makeup artistry and for having the confidence in me to deliver. To my dear friend and fellow makeup artist, Renee Fisher, for giving me opportunities that led me here. And to my mentor, Vincent Longo, who is not only a master of his craft but also a generous teacher. Many thanks.

Introduction

For as long as I can remember, I loved to color—crayons, pencils, paint, it really didn't matter. I loved it all and I was good at it. I remember distinctly being praised for my ability to "stay inside the lines," no small feat for a five-year-old, and a huge compliment since it was usually older people offering the praise. Looking back, it's no wonder I became a makeup artist; this coloring thing just kind of stuck.

My road to makeup artistry was a winding one, without a direct path and with lots of twists and turns, but I am exactly where I belong, and happy to inspire you on your road to becoming a makeup artist. It's enjoyable and rewarding, every day is different, and I can't think of anything else I'd rather be doing. Quite simply, it doesn't feel like work—it's just plain fun.

I've always been creative. I often joke that only one side of my brain works, and that's the creative side; it just comes naturally to me. My winding, twisty road to makeup artistry started in college, where I was studying for a degree in studio art. When I decided I wouldn't be able to make a living as an "artist," I changed direction and moved to a fashion design program. There was a small stint as a visual merchandiser, dressing windows for department stores, and a brief foray into garment manufacturing. I was willing to try anything so long as it was creative and I was collecting a paycheck. I was searching for the perfect fit. And like many of you, I was looking for the one thing that I could be passionate about, excel at, and make money doing—the holy grail of jobs.

I stumbled on my first job in makeup quite by accident. I was working at the cosmetics counter in the local mall, and although I didn't have any particular interest in doing makeup, per se, I thought that making a commission on the products I sold sounded like a good deal. I'd worked other retail jobs before, and none had offered me the opportunity to make a little extra money. It sure sounded like a win-win. I had no idea that this first job in cosmetics and the contacts I made there would lead to a career filled with colorful people, places, and things. It looks like the universe was in charge.

My journey truly began with a move to New York City—the Big Apple—a momentous decision for a girl from the South, with the intention of becoming . . . well, not a makeup artist. I made the move to attend New York University with the hopes of eventually becoming an occupational therapist, a far cry from where I'd been and where I would end up. Soon after arriving, I met a renowned makeup artist through a friend. He offered me a part-time job working at his newly formed cosmetics company, and what started as a part-time job while I was still a student, eventually led to a long-term position after graduation, working all facets of his business. I wore every hat imaginable as a makeup artist, from national makeup artist and account coordinator to director of training, teaching makeup artists in high-profile cosmetics stores across the country. I also started assisting him on various sets with his celebrity clientele, and the rest is history. A career was born. I learned the ins and outs of beauty, both the creative and the business side.

Once I left the retail environment and started freelancing on commercial jobs in New York, my career took off. Working behind the scenes of photoshoots and TV sets, instead of on a department store floor, showed me a completely different side of the business of makeup artistry. I honed and perfected my craft as a makeup artist, and people took notice. I started booking jobs of my own, and after a decade of working on everything from television and Broadway to runways and red carpets, I was ready to create something of my own, something over which I would have total control. I was tired of waiting for the phone to ring, tired of wondering when the next call for a job would come.

Like many of you, I was looking for a way to supplement my income and have more control over my schedule and my earnings. My intention in the beginning was to start offering lessons to women—strictly on a part-time basis, in between doing commercial jobs—but as the interest in my services grew, so did my commitment to making this adventure more than part-time.

Everything I've learned along the way has led to where I am today: the owner of my own makeup artist business. I'll share all of the knowledge I've acquired with you in the pages to follow, and walk you through the steps to opening your own business.

I opened my makeup studio in the fall of 2006, and since then, it has grown to become my full-time job. I offer customized lessons, bridal services, and a signature line of makeup. Sure, I still do commercial work—I love it, and never want to stop doing it—but opening my own makeup business has allowed me the freedom to choose the projects I want to work on and has provided more income than I had anticipated in the beginning. I have control over my schedule, my income potential, and my personal life. Most of all, I'm happy; I love what I do every day. I hope that this book will inspire you to fulfill your own dream of becoming a makeup artist.

> Makeup may not change the world or even your life, but it can be a first step in learning things about yourself you may never have discovered otherwise.
>
> —*Kevyn Aucoin*

01

So You Think You Want to be a Makeup Artist

So, now you've heard my story. The big question is, do you have what it takes? Becoming a makeup artist takes a combination of many things, but the most important requirements are artistic talent, personality, and persistence. You just won't find success in this field without possessing all of these qualities in equal measure. Artistic talent is somewhat self-explanatory, but the most successful makeup artists are artists first, and consider the face their canvas, and makeup, their paints. We use brushes as many of the great masters have done, and consider cosmetics to be our palette. You have to have the critical eye to see someone as they are along with the creative vision to see what they can become. You must understand and appreciate color, have an objective eye, and be of a visual nature. Beauty is subjective, as is any art form, and your job is to create beauty through your medium, which is makeup. No two faces are ever the same, and you have to see the beauty in every one. Possessing these qualities in perfect combination is what separates the forgettable makeup artists from the great ones.

Because the face is your canvas, and you're working one on one with someone in an intimate way, personality is a critical element to success. I would say it's just as important, if not more so, than talent. Most people will hire you the first time based on your portfolio of work, or referrals, but they will only hire you a second time if you have the personality to match. To be a successful makeup artist, you have to be a good listener; you have to be able to hear what the client wants, and be able to create a look that makes her feel comfortable and better about herself. You have to be a sleuth, a beauty detective, in order to figure out what she is looking for—what makes her feel good about herself, and what she'd like to change. Sometimes you're a friend, sometimes a therapist, sometimes a confidante. You have to be accessible, approachable, and accommodating. Remember: It's her face, not yours, and you want her to be happy. In short, you have to enjoy working closely with someone, learning all of their insecurities, and you have to want to make their day a little brighter. It's about much more than just painting.

The last quality is persistence. You have to have the guts to follow your dream and realize that your journey as a makeup artist will be unique. You have to create your own opportunities. They won't find you; you have to find them. It's what I call *the hustle*. And when an opportunity does come your way, you have to be willing to do whatever it takes to get the job done and make the client happy. You have to say yes to every opportunity that comes your way, because every door that opens leads to the next one. I can trace back almost all of the jobs I've had in the last decade or more to some of those first connections I made, as far back as that first job at the cosmetics counter in the mall. Remember, there is no job too big or too small. There is no room for ego. There's only room for hard work and persistence. The rest will follow.

Does It Pay to Go to Makeup or Beauty School?

Do you need to go to school to be a makeup artist? That's certainly a personal choice. I never formally studied makeup, nor did many of the working makeup artists that I know. Sure, I have a few formal degrees in other things, just not in makeup artistry, or even in business, for that matter, which I'm still learning as I go. With that said, there is no direct path to becoming a makeup artist. The good news about this is the fact that you get to choose whether or not you go to school. Many of the great makeup artists are self-taught visual artists, like me, who found makeup to be their ideal medium; others knew they wanted to become makeup artists from an early age, and studied at a makeup or cosmetology school. Either way, a passion for color, art, and people is a prerequisite; whether you decide to study in your own way or seek out a structured program, that's up to you. You may even decide to do both.

Let's begin by taking a look at the pros and cons of both avenues, self-taught and formal schooling.

If you're interested in learning in a structured, formal setting, then a makeup course, program, or school may be the right move for you. Almost every area of the country will have a cosmetology program that offers a makeup course. You may even find other established makeup artists in your area that offer seminars or workshops for aspiring artists. Since formal schooling is a big expense up front, be sure to ask about what type of makeup techniques the program will cover, the credentials of the instructor, and the tools and supplies that will be provided. For example, if you're interested in learning bridal makeup techniques and the course is geared toward another type of makeup artistry, you'll want to know that before you sign up. Choose your classes according to the types of makeup techniques you'd like to learn. Also, some courses may require that you already have a full makeup kit, while others may provide you with some makeup and tools, so ask what products and tools are needed beforehand. The point is, ask questions before you enroll in any course or program. It's an expense, and you want to make sure you're getting your money's worth.

Another benefit to enrolling in a makeup class or program is the opportunity to make connections and meet other makeup artists. Even today, not only do I learn new tips and tricks from my makeup artist friends, but we also recommend each other for jobs. Making those connections is a great way to get your business started. For example, if I'm fully booked already when someone requests my services, I will recommend another artist for the job, passing his contact information along to the potential client. Building a relationship with a program instructor is also beneficial. If you have a highly qualified instructor, he may be able to guide you well after the course is over, becoming your beauty ally. In short, this business is all about meeting people and making connections; what better way to do that than by starting with your peers and other like-minded professionals.

So, how do you go about learning on your own?

Well, if you already have an artistic eye, you may find this method will work for you. There are many resources online, like video tutorials and beauty blogs. You can find books by famous and established makeup artists that illustrate their techniques. And of course, there is inspiration in all of the fashion and beauty magazines. There is instruction and inspiration everywhere if you're willing to practice. You can choose to pick up books on specific techniques or styles of makeup, or you may want to experiment with a little bit of everything until you find your own particular style. Practice what you learn on your friends and family until you feel confident and their feedback is positive. Ask for honest critique and feedback from every person you touch. The downside to going it alone is that you won't make those connections and relationships with other makeup artists, and you may not have someone with a more experienced eye to guide your technique. Sometimes it's hard to be objective about your own shortcomings, and you can't always see where you may have room for improvement.

There are pros and cons to both approaches. Either way, let's review:

Makeup or Beauty School
Pros:

- You learn in a formal, structured setting.

- You get to meet other like-minded people and make connections.

- You have an instructor or other experienced artists to help guide your technique.

- You receive objective critique and feedback about your work.

Cons:

- There are monetary obligations such as tuition and/or school loans.

- You are limited to the class schedule, which may be difficult to commit to if you already have a part- or full-time job.

- The quality of the education and the techniques you learn are limited to the instruction offered at the school.

- The school's main focus may not be makeup. If it's a school that offers instruction in other services, check the credentials of the instructors who teach the makeup courses to ensure they are experienced makeup artists.

Self-Taught
Pros:

- There are no monetary obligations, like tuition or school loans.

- You can learn on your own time and at your own pace.

Cons:

- There is no feedback or critique on your work, so it's harder to compare your work to others.

- You may not be able to make as many valuable connections within the industry right away.

Artists and Their Paths to Success

As you already know, my path was a winding one, and I'm not alone. Many of the artists you're familiar with today took very different paths and run their businesses in very different ways. Let's look at the inspirational stories of a few of these artists, some who received a formal education in makeup artistry, and some who were self-taught.

Kevyn Aucoin

Kevyn Aucoin was an iconic, revered makeup artist, and even after his death in 2002, his mastery of technique and beauty philosophy lives on through his many books and his product line. Kevyn's career started after he dropped out of high school and enrolled in beauty school in his hometown of Lafayette, Louisiana. There he discovered his passion for makeup, and he was so good at it, he actually ended up teaching the class. He soon found a small corner of a women's boutique where he could practice his makeup skills. The women of Lafayette felt uncomfortable having a man do their makeup, so Kevyn moved to Baton Rouge, Louisiana, a larger city, in an attempt to realize his dream of becoming a makeup artist.

In the early 1980s, Kevyn decided to move to New York City with his then-boyfriend, Jed Root, who often acted as his manager. He started his career doing free test shoots on models, and was soon discovered by famed photographer, Steven Meisel. Numerous *Vogue* and *Cosmopolitan* covers followed, and soon A-list celebrities were requesting Kevyn's talent for photo shoots and award shows. His celebrity clients included Cher, Janet Jackson, Lisa Marie Presley, and Gwyneth Paltrow, among others.

Kevyn's best-selling books are still available for purchase (see appendix for details). Part inspiration, part instruction, they should be a part of every makeup artist's collection. He was one of the masters of our time, and we can all learn from his impeccable technique and dynamic career. You can purchase his makeup line at www.kevynaucoin.com.

> It is by celebrating the differences in others that we can begin to accept our own individuality.
>
> —*Kevyn Aucoin*

Vincent Longo: Meet My Mentor

Vincent Longo, born in Australia to Italian parents, spent his childhood surrounded by natural beauty, the foundation of his keen eye for color. As a teen, his family moved back to Italy, where Vincent started his career as a makeup artist by enrolling in a prestigious makeup school in Milan. After graduating, he began working with Italy's top designers—Gianni Versace, Dolce & Gabbana, Giorgio Armani, and Gianfranco Ferré. Known for his skills in editorial and runway, Vincent's career soon took him to New York City, where he worked with countless supermodels and celebrities, creating looks for high-profile fashion and beauty magazines like *ELLE, Vogue, Glamour,* and *Vanity Fair.*

In 1994, frustrated with the range of color available on the market, Vincent began mixing his own colors in his Manhattan apartment, and soon had requests from celebrity friends and clients for the unique shades. His makeup line was born and soon included a revolutionary product called "Water Canvas," a foundation that sparked a new industry standard. His use of color and eye for transformation has garnered Vincent Longo a cult following among those in the fashion and beauty industry. You can find out more about Vincent Longo products at www.vincentlongo.com.

I'm proud to say that Vincent Longo is my mentor. He's a generous artist with enormous creative vision, and is a remarkably open teacher. Everything I know about makeup, technique, color, retail, and business I can attribute to Vincent and his willingness to take me along on his journey. Without question, my career is what it is today because of his direction, and because he saw potential in me.

Bobbi Brown

Bobbi Brown has created a beauty and cosmetics empire—all from a small line of ten lipsticks called Bobbi Brown Essentials, launched at Bergdorf Goodman in 1991. She sold 100 lipsticks that first day, and the rest is history. Her cosmetics can be found in almost every mall across the United States and internationally.

Her journey in makeup started with a degree in theatrical makeup at Emerson College in Boston. Soon after, she moved to New York City to pursue a career as a professional makeup artist. After pounding the pavement and showing her portfolio to anyone who would take a look, Bobbi finally got a break and started working with top magazines, models, and photographers. Opportunities to work with *American Vogue, Cosmopolitan,* and *Self* came along, and Bobbi's career as a makeup artist took off.

In addition, Bobbi has authored five books (see appendix for details). Both instructional and inspirational, her books are must-haves for aspiring makeup artists. They are particularly helpful for beginners, and include how-tos and unprecedented advice. Also a supporter of the Dress for Success nonprofit organization, Bobbi donates products and time to making underprivileged women feel more beautiful and confident as they search for new jobs.

You can learn more about Bobbi Brown at www.bobbibrowncosmetics.com.

> A strong brow, bedroom eyes, a bump on the nose—these are the features that inspire me. Beauty isn't about looking perfect. It's about celebrating your individuality.
>
> —*Bobbi Brown*

Pat McGrath

Pat McGrath was raised in Northampton, England, and credits her mother for her love and interest in fashion and makeup. Pat began her career as a makeup artist with no formal training in 1990, after completing an art foundation course at Northampton College. She's often been quoted as saying, "I really love being a makeup artist. It never gets mundane or predictable, and every shoot and show is different."

Since then, she's worked with top photographers and publications around the world, including *Vogue* and *Harper's Bazaar*. She's credited with creating looks for Prada and Miu Miu, and in 1999, designed the cosmetics line for Armani. In 2004, she was named global cosmetics creative-design director for Procter & Gamble, whose product lines include Max Factor, COVERGIRL, and Dolce & Gabbana. With countless editorial and runway credits and a high-profile celebrity clientele, Pat McGrath continues to be one of the most influential makeup artists of our day.

> I'm influenced a lot by the fabrics that I see, the colours that are in the collections, and the girls' faces. It's always a challenge but that's the key—to make it different every time.
>
> —*Pat McGrath*

Best known for creating glamorous looks for African-American women, Sam Fine has a celebrity roster that includes Vanessa L. Williams and Halle Berry, along with supermodels Tyra Banks, Veronica Webb, Iman, and Naomi Campbell.

Sam Fine started his makeup career in his hometown of Chicago, selling cosmetics at the makeup counter in his local department store. He refers to his early experience as "the real school of beauty," and took the skills he learned while instructing and demonstrating on the women of Chicago to the covers of popular beauty and fashion magazines, including *Cosmopolitan, Harper's Bazaar, Essence, Vibe,* and *Marie Claire.* He was honored to be selected as the first African-American spokesperson for Revlon and COVERGIRL Cosmetics, and has penned a beauty guide designed specifically for women of color (see appendix for details).

His work and rise to the top of the industry is inspirational for every makeup artist who aspires to reach beyond the basics. You can learn more about Sam Fine and his work at www.samfine.com.

Now that you've weighed the pros and cons and heard real-life stories of makeup artists who have made it to the top, both in retail and professional freelance artistry, the decision to move forward is yours. Whichever route you decide to go, know that success can be yours either way. With passion, persistence, and hard work, you'll have the foundation you'll need to start your own makeup artist business.

Assisting: Learning by Doing

So, you've probably made a decision on whether or not to pursue formal training and are looking forward to what lies ahead as a makeup artist—but you'd like some more experience first. What's the next step? Well, there are other ways to learn and get your feet wet in addition to the ways we've already discussed; in the industry, we call it "assisting." Assisting another makeup artist is one of the best ways you can learn—and not only about the art of makeup, but also the art of interacting with clients. You get to see how that particular makeup artist relates to his clients, how he listens and handles objections, how he interprets each client's needs, and how he creates a look that's suitable for them. You get to learn what his process for application is, and even his little tips, tricks, and product suggestions. This is hands down one of the best ways to learn—from another already-successful makeup artist. It's what I did, and it's what propelled my career forward. The knowledge I gained was invaluable, both in artistry and client relations, and if there's one thing I think every aspiring makeup artist should do, it's serve as an assistant. You may find that assisting one artist is what you'd like to do, or you might like to get the perspective and experience from several different artists. There's no right or wrong way, but the more artists you assist, the more opportunity you'll have to learn what works for you and what doesn't.

How Do You Go about Assisting Another Makeup Artist?

The best thing to do is find an artist or artists in your area whose work and business you admire and ask to meet with them. I receive e-mails all the time from new and aspiring artists interested in assisting me. You may decide to send them an e-mail or give them a call; however you choose to make contact, if there's a personal connection, make sure the artists know that you're interested in volunteering your time to help them out in exchange for the opportunity to shadow them and learn in the process. Some artists may offer you money in exchange for your help, but assisting is generally unpaid work. Consider assisting an apprenticeship or internship, and an integral part of your education. Who doesn't want a free education?

What Will You Get to Do While You're Assisting?

Well, that will vary depending on the artist. You may just be shadowing her, which means coming along with her just to observe, or she may want you to actually help out. I've had other artists assist me on everything from weddings to fashion shows, or I've just agreed to meet with them, one on one, to share my story and experiences and offer advice. When you're assisting, it's important to be flexible and accommodating; no task should be too big or too small. Whatever it is, be there, be attentive, and be ready for whatever comes your way.

- Does the artist need you to find a product in his kit?
- Does he need water or coffee?
- Or is he running behind and need you to jump in and help with makeup?

You could offer to clean brushes, sharpen pencils, or tidy up his kit or workstation. Be there on call for him, and if you have time, make sure to watch him do makeup.

Take notes and study the artist's steps.

- What products is she using?
- In what order is she applying products?
- What colors has she chosen for the client, and why?
- What questions is she asking the client?
- What is her communication style?

Predict the artist's next move and watch over her shoulder as she does someone's makeup. Study the artist's technique and how she interacts with her clients, always remembering that you are there to learn.

Assisting another makeup artist also has other benefits, including networking. We'll talk more in depth about that later, but it's important to remember that networking and referrals are the backbone of this business. If the makeup artist you are assisting likes your work and the way you interact with a client, he will be more likely to recommend you if he is busy or already booked. Making a good impression on an already-successful artist is one of the best ways to get your own business started.

Learning and Practicing in a Retail Environment

There is another way to learn by doing, and that's by working in a retail environment, like the cosmetics counter of your local department store. Many of the cosmetics companies that you're familiar with hire what are called promotional or freelance makeup artists. This position is usually freelance, meaning it has flexible hours and offers a reasonable part-time income. It's a great training ground for aspiring artists, and one I would recommend exploring to see if it's a good fit for you. Most companies offer some basic training, primarily about their products and sometimes about general technique, so that is another benefit. They will generally give you samples at these trainings so you can start to build a kit of products that you love and have been trained to work with. They will also typically book appointments for you so you'll have lots of faces to practice on, and plenty of time to perfect your technique; in addition, you can often work for more than one company at a time so you'll have the benefit of learning about many different lines of makeup and have the chance to make those much-needed connections we talked about.

I know you're thinking you want to open up your own business, but the great news is, because these positions are freelance—meaning you can choose the days you work—you will still have enough time to start your own makeup business. You'll find that you will meet other makeup artists, make connections within the industry, build up clientele, learn about the products and how they perform, and make some part-time income—which is especially helpful if you are concerned about making the leap from the security of a full-time job to your own business as an independent makeup artist. This is a great way to explore makeup artistry without making a full-time commitment.

If this sounds like a good fit for you, the best place to start is by contacting the counter manager or account executive of your favorite makeup line in your local department store. Each manager or account executive should be able to give you more information about how their company's program works, who to contact, and how to apply for the position. You may also check the websites of each company for more information.

Practice, Practice, Practice

I really can't stress this enough; there's simply no replacement for it. Even after you've been to school, assisted other artists, and researched and read every book there is on makeup, practice is still the key to perfection. Every artist has to hone her craft, and makeup artistry is no different. The more opportunities you have to apply makeup, on women of a variety of ages and ethnicities, the more confident you'll be. The good news is that roughly half of the population is made up of women. There are faces everywhere. You can even practice on yourself.

I think that one of the biggest obstacles new artists face is trying to make everyone truly look like themselves. We've all applied our own makeup, but even if this look is flattering and comfortable for us, don't assume that it will be the right look on someone else. Their features and likes and dislikes will be different from yours, so practice a variety of looks on a variety of people. And don't be afraid to experiment or step outside of your comfort zone. We are thankfully not tattoo artists, just makeup artists, and makeup washes right off. If you don't like something you've applied, remove it and start again.

No one wants to be a one-trick pony, as this will be apparent in your work and your portfolio. You need to have vision and techniques for every person you encounter, and the only way to do this is to practice. Find women of all shapes, sizes, and shades to serve as your canvas. Ask if you can do their makeup for a special event, or even just a girls' night out. Find women in your circle who may just need a lift or a pick-me-up. Volunteer your services at women's groups or shelters. Bribe your friends and family. Do what you have to do to find faces to practice on.

Always have a collection of aspirational looks to practice. Collect photos from fashion, beauty, and women's magazines that suit a variety of people, and keep them in a folder as reference so you have some ideas and looks to practice when the time comes. Watch makeup tutorials on the Internet, find beauty blogs online with looks you like, or mimic your favorite celebrity looks. The point is practice, practice, and practice some more.

Self-Employment versus the Security of a Full-Time Job

Are you ready to make the leap from a full-time job to being self-employed as a makeup artist? You may or may not be, but here's the great news: You can decide! Depending on your financial needs, makeup artistry can be a full-time career choice or a part-time way to make some extra money. When I started my business, I was still working on a lot of commercial jobs in New York City. The commute was tiresome and the days on set were long. I wanted to open a business, near my home in Connecticut, where I would have control over my schedule and could have something to rely on when there were droughts in the commercial arena. In other words, I wanted to create a job and a lifestyle that I could control and that would support me. I wanted my makeup artist business to come first and the commercial work to be extra. And thankfully, that's just what I've achieved. Your goals and desire to be a makeup artist may not match mine, but you can and should structure your business any way you like, to meet both your financial needs and your personal goals as an artist. My business model works for me and yours will work for you. No two makeup artist businesses have to be the same. Like anything, the more you put into it, the more you'll get out of it.

Starting a business out of your love of makeup artistry requires patience, persistence, and hard work, just like any business. This is true whether you're a seasoned professional with a long history in the makeup industry or if you're just getting started. Most businesses don't open their doors and thrive overnight. You have to put in the work to reap the rewards, and it may take years before you see a profit. Unfortunately, you can't expect a large salary to start rolling in the minute you declare yourself a makeup artist. I know that sounds harsh, but that is the reality. If your goal is to make some extra money on the weekends, and you aren't trying to replace a full-time salary, then you may be happier with the progression of your business in the beginning than someone who is relying solely on income as a makeup artist to survive. Just be realistic with yourself. Are you someone whose happiness depends on the security of a regular paycheck? If so, you may not want to jump in headfirst; you may prefer to ease your way into this, and the great news is that you can. You can take baby steps and start your makeup artist business as a part-time venture, and decide later on where you'd like it to go from there.

Since the majority of the work you'll do as a makeup artist can be scheduled on weekends, it makes it much easier to start your own business on a part-time basis. Most women book their beauty services for the weekend, including brides, so if you're uncomfortable taking a big leap, you can start your business part-time on the weekends and still have the security of a full-time job during the week. You can also start at your own pace and control the amount of work you accept. You'll know when the time is right to move forward and grow your business, or not.

Seasonality in Your Region and Other Considerations

So you've decided to take the plunge. You've decided to go for it. What do you have to lose? Honestly, nothing. You have everything to gain. But before you get too excited and start announcing that you're a makeup artist, there are a few things to consider, like:

- Where do you live?
- What type of makeup work will be available to you?
- Do you live in a rural area or a bustling city?
- Do you live in an area where the majority of the women wear makeup on a regular basis, or in an area where makeup is saved for special occasions?
- Is your community a resort town?

As you can see, there are lots of things to consider before you get started. Your opportunities as a makeup artist will be based on where you live. That's just a cold, hard fact.

If your goal is to be a high-profile makeup artist in the world of beauty, fashion, and celebrity, then you have to live in areas where those opportunities exist, like New York City or Los Angeles. But if your goal and interest in makeup artistry is to help real women look and feel their best, then you can do that anywhere! Roughly 55 percent of the nation's population is made up of women over the age of eighteen. That's 150 million women who most likely want to look and feel their best, and that doesn't even include the teen population. Now, quite obviously, all of those women don't live in your city or town, and they all won't be your clients, but you get the idea.

There's no shortage of potential. I've had clients as young as age twelve for birthday parties and women as mature as eighty, looking for advice and real answers to their makeup questions. Women never stop wanting to look their best. Whether you're giving introductory makeup lessons or handling brides and bridal parties, all women love a little expert advice when it comes to beauty. So when you're thinking about your new business as a makeup artist, take some time to think about who your client is and what types of services she might like.

Another consideration is also seasonality. Your income and opportunities may also be limited by, quite simply, the weather. For example, in the Northeast, the majority of brides get married between April and October, which leaves five months of the year without that income to rely on. If you're lucky enough to live in milder climates, you may enjoy the benefit of having more bridal clients on a year-round basis. I also offer makeup lessons, which seem to be the most popular in the spring and the fall when women are changing their look with the seasons. So you can see, you have to consider how your business will look throughout the year.

Do you live in a resort town? Is your potential clientele only there during the high seasons? Are you in an area known for destination weddings, or do you live in a rural community where women wear minimal makeup? The point is, do your research. Find out who your client base is and when they will most be in need of your services, and then tailor your business to suit those parameters.

You've thought about it, and thought about it some more, and you've finally decided to make the leap. You're ready to get started in your new career as a makeup artist. But before you can start any kind of business, you need a place to work out of and the right tools and equipment to work with. You need an office. And where's the easiest, most convenient place to set up shop? Right in your own home. Let's walk through the steps and equipment you'll need to put together a productive home office.

Setting Up a Home Office

Everyone needs a space to call her own, even if you're a freelance makeup artist. You'll need to set up a space where you can handle all of your business matters outside of the makeup artistry itself. Tracking sales, fielding inquiries, answering e-mails, and returning phone calls, your home office will be your business "storefront." For a makeup artist business, this is easy and doesn't require much more equipment than you probably already own. Outside of the usual items like pens, paper, paper clips, file folders, and a stapler, I chose to use my already-existing equipment, like my existing landline and computer. It's economical, and cuts back on out-of-pocket expenses in the beginning.

You'll want to set up your home office in an area where you can work, undisturbed by spouses, children, pets, and the blare of the television, preferably someplace where you can shut the door behind you and "close your business" when the end of the day comes. What will you need in your home office? Let's take a look at some of the required equipment for a productive, organized workspace.

Computer

Most people already have a computer, if not more than one, in their household. If you don't, you'll need to invest in one. I do all of my non–makeup artistry work on the computer, including marketing, accounting, and more. Depending on your household, you may be sharing a computer with a spouse, children, or friends, and don't have a computer that can be dedicated just for business use. If that's the case, you may consider negotiating specific hours that you can use the computer uninterrupted. Create computer "business hours," so to speak.

And if you're still living in the dark ages and don't have high-speed Internet of some kind, you'll need to get that as soon as possible. It will be impossible to surf the Internet, do your market research, download photos and upload them to your website or blog, and operate efficiently without it. If you need to upgrade, I'd suggest purchasing the highest speed connection you can afford. All of your marketing efforts will originate from your computer, so make sure that your connection is strong and fast. You can obtain high-speed Internet through your cable company or phone-service provider. If you're in a rural area, you can often get high-speed service through a satellite dish. Do a Google search for "high-speed Internet" in your area and the providers and options available to you will pop right up. Find a plan that suits your budget and needs.

All-In-One Printer

You should also have an all-in-one printer, which means it does everything from copying and printing to scanning and faxing. You'll need the copy feature to make copies of contracts and invoices. It has a printing feature, including color, which allows you to print your marketing materials, directions to locations, and contracts. It also allows you to scan, which comes in handy if you want to scan photos of makeup work that you've done or other materials to upload to a blog. You can even receive faxes on it. It's a handy all-in-one tool. They are reasonably priced, can be purchased online or at your local office supply store, and will make your work more centralized and much easier to manage.

Software

Most computers come with some sort of basic word processing program. Believe it or not, several simple programs on your computer are all you will need to get started; you can add more-advanced programs as your business grows.

Word Processing and Spreadsheets

I've purchased two computers in the last several years, one a desktop and one a laptop. Both have come with some sort of word processing program that allows you to write documents and has basic programs like simple spreadsheets and calendars, which will be helpful in scheduling and tracking clients. Most of the advanced programs, like Microsoft Word, offer more, but you also have to pay extra to install it onto your computer. If you're already using something like Microsoft Word, you should have all you need to get started. If you don't have Microsoft Word or something similar already installed on your computer, and you don't want to invest in more software, consider looking into OpenOffice. For many moons, I was using Microsoft Works, which was already installed on my computer, but I was having trouble opening files and editing them. OpenOffice offers the same basic programs offered on Microsoft Word, and I am now able to open any document without a problem. Plus, the download and installation are free. You can find out more about it at www.openoffice.org. You might need to upgrade to a more-comprehensive accounting software, like QuickBooks, as your business grows, but these basic programs will get you started. You can get more information and pricing at www.quickbooks.intuit.com.

Google Docs

Google Docs is another option if you're considering a word processing program. It's similar to other office suites in that your documents can be saved directly onto your computer, but your documents will also be automatically saved to Google's server. The benefit is that you always have access to your files online, even with an app on your phone, and you won't have the worry of losing your documents. They'll always be backed up. You can even import existing documents that you already have. The basic package is free, but you can upgrade at minimal cost. You can learn more at www.docs.google.com.

PhotoScape

I've also found the PhotoScape program to be very useful, especially in building my online portfolio, and I highly recommend installing it on your computer. PhotoScape is another free program that lets you edit and alter photographs, much like a simple version of Photoshop, which many professional photographers use in editing their photos. As photographers started sending me images of my work to include in my portfolio, I noticed that the files they were sending me were too large to upload to my blog or social media sites. With PhotoScape, I can size the photos myself to the site requirements without asking the photographer to resize them for me. I've also been able to create inspirational storyboards for photo shoots and create some basic marketing materials using the photos of my work. You can download PhotoScape for free by going to www.photoscape.org.

Phone

So, do you need a separate business phone? Well, this is actually a trickier subject than it sounds. You can choose to use an already-existing phone line, like your home or office line, or you could use your cell-phone number. The truth is, we all have multiple phone lines already. Is it more work to add another one into the mix? I personally have both a landline and a cell phone. I wasn't using my landline very often, so I decided to use that number as my business phone. It was already conveniently located in my home office, and to be completely honest, I didn't want to pay for another phone every month. In the beginning, I also gave some clients my cell-phone number.

The problem is, now that my business has grown, I have clients calling both numbers, which means I have to stay on top of both phones, not to mention two e-mail addresses and the occasional text message or direct message on Facebook or Twitter. It's a lot to manage. The other important thing you want to consider if you don't have a dedicated business line is whether you want your home and personal messages combined with business ones. This certainly depends on your circumstances, but it's something worth thinking about. There are so many inexpensive phone plans now, with both cell and landlines available through your Internet service provider, it's a reasonable option to have a phone dedicated just to your business. As it grows you'll be happy that you did.

What about 1-800 numbers? In my opinion, a 1-800 number isn't necessary. As a makeup artist, you are servicing clients in your immediate area for the most part, and having a local phone prefix makes more sense. Clients actually like to know that you're local when they're shopping around for someone.

Another option is hiring a phone service called an auto-attendant. These services start as low as $25 per month. They'll answer the phone number of your choice in person for you and relay the client's message to you, in any manner you like, be it text message, e-mail, or phone. The benefit is, there's always someone there to answer the phone for you. It's a much more personal client experience than leaving a message.

Calculator

I know this sounds so remedial and basic, but I can't tell you how many times I've returned a call from a potential client only to have them request a quote for bridal services or want to purchase some makeup, and I've had to scramble around, looking for a calculator. I've already confessed that one side of my brain works overtime, the creative side, while the other side remains relatively dormant. So if you're not a math whiz, I'd suggest keeping a calculator nearby so you're ready with a prompt and accurate answer when someone asks, "How much?"

Creating a Home Makeup Studio

You may want to consider dedicating a space in your home as a makeup studio, possibly an extra room or barely used space, where you can work and meet with clients one on one, on your own terms. The first few clients that were referred to me came to my home for their makeup application. I quickly learned that an in-home studio wouldn't work for me, and that I would need to find a studio space outside of my home. But many of you may already have the perfect place within your home to get started. Of course, you can always meet clients at their homes or the location of their choice, but creating a home studio, if you have the room, is another option. I know another makeup artist who, instead of leasing a separate space, chose to add an addition on to her home to service her clients. This is obviously a major expense and one you may not want to take on in the beginning, but there are many options and ways to create a comfortable environment for your clients, should you choose to service them in your home.

If you choose to create a home studio, make sure the space is warm and inviting and reflects your personality and personal style. I love everything vintage, so my makeup studio (and my home) is decorated with an eclectic mix of antiques and vintage finds. Whether your style is modern or vintage, make sure to infuse your personality into the space. And, most importantly, you'll want to make sure you and the client are comfortable. Consider getting a director's chair or barstool that's a comfortable height for you to work, preferably one with a back so the client can relax. There's nothing worse for your back than bending over to do someone's makeup. You'll also need a workspace for your brushes, products, and kit. I found a vintage vanity for my studio, but any tabletop or flat surface will work. Again, make sure it's a comfortable height. And last but not least, you'll need to have proper lighting installed. The best place to do makeup is always in natural light, so if you have the luxury of setting up near a window, that's ideal. Even so, you should also consider installing lighted makeup mirrors or overhead lighting for days when there is limited natural light.

Also be mindful of the fact that if clients must enter your home makeup studio through the rest of your home, the impression it makes is a significant one. If you run a hustling, bustling household during certain hours, only schedule makeup clients when it's calm and quiet, and the surroundings are tidy and organized.

Becoming a Certified Makeup Artist

This is a tricky and contentious question in my book. In my mind, getting a "certification" in makeup doesn't necessarily make you a good makeup artist. Anyone can enroll, take a course, and get their certificate, which essentially just shows that you paid for, attended, and completed the course. In my mind, there's no real way to certify talent; you either have it or you don't. And don't forget—you have to have the personality and persistence to match your talent, and there's no way to certify either of those. As my friend put it, there's no PhD of makeup artistry. If you do earn a certificate from a program or course you attended, then certainly that's a good thing, and if you don't have any certificates to add to your résumé, don't be discouraged; being "certified" isn't a requirement for success.

Do You Need a Cosmetology License?

This is a question without an easy or straightforward answer. I know you're looking for a "yes" or "no," but each state has its own laws regarding the licensure of beauty professionals, including makeup artistry. Although many of you may have "certifications," a state license is something altogether different, and may or may not be required by your state in order for you to start your own makeup artist business.

Many states include makeup artistry under the umbrella of aesthetics (the study of skincare and facial treatments) so a license in aesthetics may be required where you live. In addition, some states may have restrictions on mobile beauty services, including spas, salons, and independent beauty professionals, which may impact your ability to service clients at their homes. Should your state require some sort of license, you generally must have a high school diploma and be over a certain age to apply. Licensing also requires a certain number of hours of instruction, and you must pass both written and practical tests administered by a State Board of Examiners. Unfortunately, certifications you've earned through enrollment or achievement in makeup artist classes, workshops, or schools aren't transferable, and won't apply toward licensing should it be required.

The only way to know for sure if licensing is required in your area is to visit the website of your State Board of Cosmetology. Or you can visit this comprehensive online listing at: www.beautytech.com/st_boards.htm.

LLC and Other Legal Matters

Another thing to consider when you're opening your business is your business structure from a legal standpoint. You want to make sure that you are protected in any legal situation that should arise. In addition to the legal considerations, choosing a business structure will also affect your taxes.

So how do you make sure you protect yourself and your business?

There are two options that might be appropriate for a home-based makeup artist business: sole proprietorship and LLC, otherwise known as a limited liability company or corporation.

Sole Proprietorship

Let's start by looking at the easiest form of business structure, and that is a sole proprietorship. A sole proprietorship is a one-person business, and, unlike an LLC, is not registered with the state. The easiest part of setting one up is that there is nothing to do. You don't have to file any papers with the state or draft any particular paperwork in order to establish yourself as a business. You simply just declare that you are going into business for yourself.

What this means from a legal standpoint is that there is no distinction between you and your business. In the eyes of the law, you are considered one and the same. This means that you report all of your income from your business on your personal tax return and are personally liable for any business-related obligations, such as debts or court judgments.

Because this is the easiest way to start your business, this may be the best option for you, provided you are comfortable being personally liable for any situations that might arise from a tax and legal standpoint.

Let's look at another option, an LLC, or limited liability company.

LLC

The primary difference between a sole proprietorship and an LLC is that the LLC separates the business owner from the business itself. From a legal standpoint, this means the business is a completely separate legal and tax entity, thus limiting your liability as the business owner. In short, your personal affairs and your business are viewed separately in the eyes of the law. Because of this, owners of an LLC don't file on their personal tax returns. The business itself pays these taxes. Owners only pay personal income tax on money they earn from the business.

LLCs also provide limited personal liability for business debts and claims. An LLC might be the best option for you if you plan on borrowing money or taking out loans from creditors to open your business, or if you have substantial personal assets that may be at risk should you be sued.

If you've decided an LLC is the right direction for you, you can easily have the paperwork drafted by an attorney. If you already have a trusted lawyer, you may look to them for advice first; if you don't have a lawyer, you can use an online service, like www.legalzoom.com. Another option may be your local university or law school. Many law schools have programs where students will draft basic legal documents for small businesses and individuals at no cost.

Do You Need a Tax ID Number?

A federal tax ID number, otherwise known as an Employer Identification Number (EIN), is essentially a social security number for your business, and in some circumstances it will benefit you to have one. Once you've decided whether to conduct your business as a sole proprietorship or an LLC, you can decide how you'd like to proceed. If you are the sole member and owner of your business—meaning you don't have any business partners or employees—then you don't need a separate EIN to conduct business. It's not required in a sole proprietorship or LLC where there is only one person. If you have gone into business with a friend or partner, or if you plan to hire employees at some point, then a separate EIN would be required. If you're unsure how to proceed, it's best to contact a tax or legal professional. For more information, you can also visit www.info.legalzoom.com.

Insurance

Opening your own business also means that you're responsible for being properly insured. There are several types of insurance you might want to consider based on your plans for your business.

Health

The first type of insurance you'll need if you aren't already covered on someone else's policy is health insurance. If you've been working at a full-time job that supplied all of your benefits, including health care, this may sound like a large expense, but there are many affordable options out there for freelancers. Because each state is different in terms of the companies, rates, and policies available, searching the Internet for "health insurance for self-employed (in your state)" will lead you to online portals and individual companies and brokers that can find you a policy that works for you and your family. You may also consider visiting a local insurance agent for more details and explanations about coverage.

Insuring Your Kit

Another thing to consider is insuring your makeup kit. Once you've amassed thousands of dollars' worth of products, brushes, and other tools, putting together your dream kit, it would be very sad to discover that it had been stolen from a venue or your car, or that it was lost in a fire or flood. You just never know what's going to happen in this crazy world, so protecting what is essentially your bread and butter only makes good sense. The first step is checking with your home and automobile insurance carriers to find out what type of protection you already have, and, if necessary, what extra coverage or riders you can add to protect your kit.

If your current policies don't cover your makeup kit, you may need to look into other options. Unfortunately, some homeowner's policies don't cover equipment and supplies related to a home-based business, so you'll need to purchase a separate policy to protect your business assets. You might want to explore the idea of purchasing commercial property insurance, particularly an "all risks policy," which may cover everything from theft or damage to your kit to "business interruption," should you lose any income due to the loss of your kit. To find out your best options for coverage, consult with your local insurance professional.

Tracking Travel and Mileage

Another consideration, and an important one at that, is whether you own a car. As a makeup artist, you'll be traveling here and there, to and fro, meeting with clients in their homes or their preferred locations, making them look their very best, and you'll need a reliable car to get you there and back. Depending on where you live, public transportation may be available, and in certain cities, like New York City, Washington,

D.C., or Boston, it will certainly get you where you need to go. But keep in mind: You'll be carting a case of makeup with you. Trust me, it will be heavy and cumbersome, and traveling to clients in your car will make your life much easier, especially if you live in areas where public transportation isn't as extensive. If you're in a suburb or rural area, make sure your wheels are in good repair and always gassed up and ready to go.

If your business is thriving, that means you'll be driving, driving, driving, and logging many miles on your car's odometer. The good news is, all—or a portion of—those miles and other car-related expenses can be deducted on your tax return. The IRS sets a rate every year for each mile you drive for business-related purposes. Keeping track of those miles can be cumbersome, but knowing that you might be getting some of that money back should make the inconvenience worth the effort.

In addition to your mileage expenses, your gasoline and car maintenance and repair expenses can often be written off on your taxes, so keep all of your car-related receipts. If you're using public transportation, keep all the receipts for monthly passes, tokens, taxis, and any other forms of transportation.

Saving Receipts and Tax Deductions

In addition to the mileage and car-related expenses discussed above, there is a number of other items that will be tax-deductible. As a self-employed makeup artist, the IRS allows deductions for a variety of business expenses. We'll take a look at some of the items you may be able to deduct. Save your receipts for:

- **Makeup and beauty supplies:** Makeup, brushes, tools, lashes, brush cleanser, and all the items you use to stock your kit. If it goes in your kit, keep a receipt for it.

- **Office supplies:** Computer, printer, software, paper, pens, organizers, and any other item you purchase to set up your home-based office.
- **Education:** Any expenses for workshops, seminars, cosmetology schools, and textbooks. This covers enrollment in any class related to your business.
- **Accountant and attorney fees:** The fees you pay your accountant or attorney for business-related services may be tax-deductible.
- **Travel:** Mileage, gas, car repairs and maintenance, parking, airfare, and public transportation costs. If you are traveling as a makeup artist, your travel costs are deductible.
- **Food:** In certain circumstances, meals are deductible. If you are having a work-related meal, save your receipts.
- **Grooming:** A portion of professional clothing, shoes, haircuts, nail grooming, and any other expenses related to personal grooming and appearance may be deductible.
- **Insurance:** Health, life, automobile, and business insurance—any insurance you carry may be deductible.
- **Medical:** Medical expenses, prescriptions, and dental.
- **Promotional:** Postcards, business cards, brochures—any materials you create to promote yourself.
- **Research:** Fashion and beauty magazines, movies and movie rentals, books, and theater.
- **Communication:** Home phone, cell phone, Internet service, and long-distance plans.
- **Donations and gifts:** This may include any product or service you donate to charitable organizations or events.
- **Home:** If you are a homeowner, home insurance, home maintenance, repair and upgrades, as well as property tax.
- **Utilities:** Gas, water, electricity, and oil.

This is just a sampling of the items that may be tax-deductible. Because everyone's tax situation is unique, it's best to consult your tax professional for the items that apply to you. Your accountant should be able to supply you with a list of items that will guide you throughout the year. When in doubt, save the receipt.

03

Make a Plan of Action

I know you're excited and ready to get going, but any well-thought-out business starts with a solid plan, a road map to success. You need to know who your audience is, where to find them, and how to get and keep their attention. You're the Girl Scout of Beauty, fully prepared for any situation that lies ahead. Why? Because you took the time to map out your plan. You'll need to ask some hard questions and make sure you know the answers before moving forward. Let's start by walking through the questions you need to ask yourself to nail down the beauty needs of your potential client base.

Research Your Region

We've touched on this before, but researching the makeup needs in your area is crucial in deciding what services to offer and how to get started. You can't jump into the game without knowing who the other players are and what is working and not working in your area. Here are some questions to ask yourself when starting your research:

- What is the demographic of the women in your area? How old are they? Are they young twentysomethings in a bustling college town, or are they moms on the go? What is their income level? Do they have disposable income? What are their ethnic and cultural concerns? Are they brides?
- Where do women in your area currently go to buy makeup or get makeup services? Do they frequent department stores, or are they purchasing makeup from the drugstore? Do they prefer home-based sales like Mary Kay or Avon? Do they schedule beauty services at the local salon or day spa?
- What are the popular makeup brands in the area? Do women in your area like new and trendy lines of makeup, or the classic tried-and-true lines?

- Are there other established freelance or self-employed makeup artists in your area? If so, what services and products do they offer?
- When do the majority of the brides in your area get married?
- Do most brides book their wedding-day makeup services at the local salon, or do they prefer service providers that come to them the day of the wedding, such as mobile spas, hair stylists, or makeup artists?
- Where are the most popular places to get your makeup done for a night out or special event (non-bridal)—the local makeup counter or day spa?
- Are there any beauty-service providers that offer birthday or bachelorette parties? Or do they offer in-home makeup parties?
- Are there times of the year that may be affected by seasonal concerns (e.g., resort towns, vacation areas, harsh winters)?

You would start your research on the Internet. Never before has there been such an immense amount of information available at your fingertips. Most makeup artists will have websites that you can visit so you can start to get an idea of what services are already offered in your area—but don't limit yourself to just makeup artists. Check out the websites of popular salons and spas. Many of them also offer makeup services, so it's important to know that as well. While you're looking at each website, make sure to take notice of the following items:

- What services does the artist offer?
- What are her rates?
- What is her background as an artist?
- Do you like the pictures and imagery?
- Does the site make you feel confident in the artist's skills?
- Would you hire this person if you were looking for a makeup artist?

Pay close attention to how the website makes you feel, and make a list of all of the things you like and don't like. You should start to get a feel for where your website should go and which services you should offer.

Don't just limit your research to the Internet. Look in local newspapers and magazines for advertisements; visit local spas or salons; call other makeup artists and ask to make appointments with them to find out how they got started. Ask friends and family where they go for makeup services. Get out there and find out what your opportunities may be.

It's also important to know if no one in your area is doing makeup or offering makeup services. That's a possibility, and if that's the case, you'll want to ask yourself why that is. Is there a need to be filled and a lot of opportunity for you, or does this mean there is no demand in your immediate area? Either way, this is important information to have.

Put Together a Business Plan

Everyone needs a plan, and writing yours down on paper is one of the first steps in clarifying what your business will look like. Most business plans are created for those who are looking for funding to start a business, or to grow an existing business, and depending on your circumstances, that may be the case for you. But even if you're planning to start your makeup artist business with your savings or out of your own pocket, writing a solid business plan will make the process of getting started a smoother one.

The basics of a business plan will vary based on your specific business idea, but a good resource for getting started is the Small Business Administration (www.sba.gov). This site walks you through the necessary steps in writing a plan. Although there is no right or wrong way to write a business plan, and yours may not fit neatly into the suggested model, this is a good resource for getting started. Here are a few of the components you will need for your business plan:

- **Executive summary:** This is the first part of your business plan and serves as an overview of your business. It should state the direction and purpose of your business. It should be concise and to the point. This is a brief summary of the sections to follow. You should also include your business contact information here, including name, phone number, address, and intended hours of operation.
- **Market analysis:** This is an overview of what is happening in your market. Are there other makeup artists in your area? What products and services are they offering? This is a section to compare and contrast what services and products are already available and where your business will fit in.
- **Marketing and sales:** In this section you should outline and discuss your strategy to find and retain clients through marketing efforts, self-promotion, and sales.
- **Products or services offered:** You want to outline the services and products that you'll be offering in this section, including how they are different from other already-existing makeup artist businesses, and what will make your services unique.

A more-comprehensive description of each section is available at www.sba.gov. You can find the section "Writing a Business Plan" by hovering over the "Starting and

Managing a Business" section in the top of the navigation bar. Another great resource is the website www.entrepreneur.com/businessplan/, which offers additional direction and even some sample business plans, including one for a hair and beauty salon.

Create a Marketing Strategy

Now, this is huge! You need a marketing strategy before you ever "open your doors," so to speak. If no one knows you're out there and available to do their makeup, then what's the point?

First you have to decide what type of client you're targeting. Is she the hip, young twentysomething looking for the latest trends, or the soccer mom who has limited time to do her makeup in the morning? Is she a retiree or a bride? Does she have disposable income? Is she a high-end client or the everyday woman on a limited budget? Make a list of the qualities you think your client may have. Does she live in your immediate area, or will she be traveling to you? Are you targeting brides, and, if so, how far will you be willing to travel?

When I was determining how I was going to market myself, I knew that I would be serving high-end clients that most likely had disposable income and would be willing to travel for my services. Thankfully, I was right about who would be attracted to my services. Women from several states have come to me for makeup lessons, and my services have become a destination. I also market my bridal services in three states, all with different bride profiles. So you see, you have to identify who will be your client before you put together a comprehensive strategy for reaching her. So, how do you start spreading the word?

Friends and Family

The first and most obvious way is to tell all of your friends and family, the ones who love and support you the most and know what you're capable of. They know your talents and strengths and your passion for makeup, so this is a no-brainer. They can be your cheerleaders and tell their friends, family, and coworkers how great you are and help to spread the word. Remember, you never know where opportunities may come from, so this is a great place to start getting referrals.

Get Business Cards

Again, another simple idea, but you never know who you'll meet, so when you meet someone new or you make a new acquaintance or friend, make sure to give them a business card. Even if you don't think they need makeup personally, you never know who they know. For example, you may meet your friend's boss, a male, at a company function. Clearly he doesn't need makeup, but your services may be a great holiday gift for his wife, or his daughter may be getting married next summer. Makeup is a very specific service for a very specific client. Trust me, they will keep your business card and call you when the time comes. (See chapter 6, "Branding Yourself," for more information on business cards.)

Reach Out to Other Businesses

Let other small business owners know that you are open for business. Target businesses that cater to women or may have women as their client base—basically, anywhere women shop or have services done. Here are some suggestions of businesses you might approach:

- Hair salons and stylists
- Manicurists and nail salons
- Personal trainers and gyms
- Day spas, cosmetic centers, and plastic surgeons
- Weight-loss centers
- Day-care centers and play groups
- Clothing boutiques, image consultants, and shoe stores
- Wedding vendors, including wedding planners, photographers, venues, and florists
- Bridal boutiques
- Gift shops
- Cafes and coffee shops
- Other small businesses run and owned by women

Remember not to limit your thinking. Women are everywhere, and now isn't the time to be shy. Stop by businesses that interest you and introduce yourself to the owner and staff. Make postcards and ask if you can leave a few for them to pass out to clients. Create a professional-looking e-mail to send out to them, or put together a press kit you can mail to people you'd like to connect with. All of these things are easy and inexpensive for you to create. (See chapter 6, "Branding Yourself," and chapter 7, "Marketing," for more information.) You'll be surprised at how supportive small business owners are of other small business owners. Some of my greatest allies and sources of referrals are the connections I made with the owners of the other businesses listed above.

Identifying and Finding Your Client

What is the average age of your client? (circle one)

18–25   25–35   35–50   55–70   70+

Does your client have disposable income? Yes ____ No ____

Choose the best description of your client:

She's working her way through school and splurges on makeup occasionally.

She's a young, hip trendy girl with money to spend on herself.

She's a working mom and watches her finances closely.

She's a working professional with a steady income.

She's well taken care of, and money isn't an issue.

She's retired and enjoying her golden years.

Describe the client/s in your area:_____

What is her lifestyle? (circle one or more)

Young and trendy   Working professional   Mom on the go

Glamorous party girl   Sophisticated and elegant   Other: _____

Does she live in _____? (circle one)

A city or metropolitan area   The suburbs   A rural community   A vacation resort

How much time does she have for makeup each day? _____

Does she wear makeup every day, or just for special occasions? _____

Where do women in your area shop for makeup? (circle one or more)

Drugstore or discount store   Department store   Specialty boutique

Spa or salon   Home party

List the stores where women can purchase makeup in your area: _____

_____

What makeup lines are the most popular with your intended client? _____

_____

Is your intended client a bride? Yes ____ No ____

Are there cultural considerations in your area? If so, list: _____

_____

Scouting the Competition

Are there other freelance makeup artists in your area? Name the artists: _____

_____

What services do they offer? (circle all that apply)

Bride and Bridal Party   Makeup Lessons (Individual)

Group Lessons or Seminars   Makeup for Special Occasions

Makeup Bag Makeover   Personal Makeup Shopping Services

In-Home Makeup Parties   Bachelorette Parties

Girls' Night Out

List additional services: _____

How much do they charge for each service? _____

List the price range in your area (Example: low end to high end, $100–$200)

Bride and Bridal Party $_____

Makeup Lessons (Individual) $_____

Group Lessons or Seminars $_____

Makeup for Special Occasions $_____

Makeup Bag Makeover $_____

Personal Makeup Shopping Services $_____

In-Home Makeup Parties $_____

Bachelorette Parties $_____

Girls' Night Out $_____

Are the artists in your area experienced or beginners? _____

_____

What strengths do you have that set you apart from the other artists in your area? _____

_____

Which artist(s) in your area do you admire, and why? _____

_____

Reaching Out to Your Client

List the businesses in your area where your client may shop:

Hair salons and stylists

_____

Manicurists and nail salons

_____

Personal trainers and gyms   • Answer is Fitness —   • Lisa's gym

Day spas, cosmetic centers, and plastic surgeons

_____

Weight-loss centers

_____

Day-care centers and play groups
   Mel

Clothing boutiques, image consultants, and shoe stores

_____

Wedding vendors, including wedding planners, photographers, venues, and florists
• Jen   • Conte

Bridal boutiques

_____

Gift shops
   • Joe DaSilva

Cafes and coffee shops

_____

List other small businesses run and owned by women in your area

_____

_____

_____

04

The Makeup Kit

Now that we've set up a home base, a place for you to successfully reach out to clients and market yourself, you'll need to put together the real tools of the trade—your makeup kit. And if you're anything like me, this is the fun part. Most of you have probably already started a collection of makeup, whether it's for your own personal use or you've been thinking ahead toward the time you could launch your own makeup artist business. Your kit is a reflection of you. It represents your style of artistry and your personal beauty philosophy. You need to make sure you know the finishes, textures, and performance of every product in your kit. What is its wearability? Who is this product suitable for? There should be a good reason for every color and every product in your kit. And because you're the Girl Scout of Beauty, you need to have shades and a range of color for every face you meet. Your kit should be a well-thought-out treasure chest of makeup magic. Let's get started. I'll walk you through some of my own personal makeup tips and tricks and make some product suggestions to launch you on your road to success.

Traditional Makeup versus Airbrush Makeup

We're all familiar with the tried-and-true way of applying makeup, but there are two ways to apply makeup these days, one of them somewhat new to the scene. Most of us use traditional makeup, meaning the kind applied with a brush, but there is also makeup that is airbrushed on using a small machine. It sprays small particles of color onto the skin and is becoming increasingly popular with makeup artists, especially within the bridal industry. If you've been to a cosmetology or makeup school, then you may be familiar with both methods and may already know which method you prefer working with. As most artists will tell you, there are pros and cons to both. Because they are different in application, you may choose to offer one or both, depending on your preference and the demand in your market.

The airbrush machine was created in response to the advent of high-definition television. Studio makeup at the time was heavy and cakey, and the industry was looking for a better way to create makeup coverage for TV personalities without it looking heavy on camera. The popularity of the airbrush grew within the industry and has now become popular in the bridal market, touting coverage that feels light and is long-lasting. I personally don't use an airbrush. It's not a tool I've ever used in my commercial or bridal work. I'm happy with the results I get using traditional makeup and brushes. However, if you're interested in airbrush makeup and the features it provides, let's take a look.

- **Investment:** Airbrush machines are an investment, especially when you're starting your own business and have so many other out-of-pocket expenses. And while the airbrush machine is primarily used for spraying on foundation, you still may want brushes to apply the rest of the color (eyes, cheeks, lips). A full set of traditional brushes, including a quality foundation brush, while an investment in itself, can be a much more economical option and come in a variety of price points. Whether you choose to airbrush or not, you'll still need a set of brushes, so if you're on a tight budget, you can choose to add the airbrush machine at a later time.
- **Finish:** Not all foundations are created equally, not even ones that are sprayed on. While the airbrush foundations come in a variety of shades, the airbrush finish may not be suitable for all skin types. One positive factor is that because of its durability and capacity to create full coverage, it's ideal for covering tattoos and other extreme skin discolorations. This comes in handy for brides who want to cover any tattoos for their big day.
- **Wearability:** Airbrush makeup is also known to be long-wearing and will stay put, with no fading throughout the day. It can last up to twenty-four hours, which is an appealing aspect for brides who have long days ahead of them.
- **User-friendliness:** One downside is, once the airbrush makeup is applied, it may be difficult for women to touch up on their own. If you're using traditional makeup, it's easier for a client to keep her look fresh with minor touch-ups throughout the day.

In my opinion, a good makeup artist can paint a beautiful face whether they're using an airbrush machine or traditional makeup. The tool is less important than the critical, creative eye and vision of the artist. I've chosen not to offer airbrush makeup and am happy only offering traditional makeup. If you're planning on offering makeup lessons to women, you'll obviously want to use traditional makeup so they can re-create their new look at home, and both purchase and work with the products you suggest. If you're considering just offering bridal services, you may want to offer both airbrush and traditional makeup. It's your personal choice as an artist; only you can decide which method is appropriate for your business and clientele, or if you'd like to offer both. You can be successful with whichever method you choose.

> Makeup is a way for a woman to look and feel like herself,
> only prettier and more confident.
>
> —*Bobbi Brown*

Investing in a Makeup Kit

Now let's put together a makeup kit. You have to have a makeup kit, and it has to have products for every type of client. You never know who you'll be working with, and you have to be prepared for every face you meet. You'll need a rainbow of colors and shades and a wide variety of products, something for everyone.

You can start to build your kit slowly, but you really won't be able to work effectively as an artist until you have a full kit. Your kit is your bread and butter. When you're choosing makeup for your kit, consider that the products you choose should reflect the tastes of the market you are serving. Does your area support a high-end clientele? If so, they are most likely expecting the products in your kit to reflect their tastes. Or is your clientele hip and trendy and expecting the newest products on the market? When you start shopping for your kit, keep these things in mind. If your clientele is in a remote area, where makeup choices are few and far between, then you may consider having brands in your kit, like Mary Kay or Avon, that can be purchased most readily and from anywhere.

Ask your friends and women in your area which products they use in order to get a sense of the products you may want to include in your kit. You may find that you can mix a variety of products, both high-end and drugstore brands. Also, don't forget that you are the expert, so don't be afraid to introduce your clients to something new. They may welcome a change from their usual routine and insider beauty tips from a professional like you.

I personally think a great makeup artist is a great makeup artist, no matter what products they choose to use. An artist should be able to make a client look beautiful no matter what, whether they are using products that are high-end and pricey or budget-friendly. The brand name is much less important than the effectiveness of the products. You just need to ask, "Does that product work for the client and meet her beauty needs?"

Certainly when you're putting your kit together, there are places where you will want to splurge and other places where you can save. I suggest your biggest splurge should be on primer, foundation, and a few special eye shadow colors. Save on mascara, eyeliner pencils, sheer lip glosses, and lipsticks. The bottom line is, fill your kit with products that perform, that you love working with, and that will appeal to your client.

Many of the makeup lines, such as MAC, offer discounts to professional, working makeup artists. Although each makeup line will have different requirements, most will require proof that you are a professional makeup artist, like a business card, license, or portfolio. Contact each company to find out if they offer any discounts, and don't forget that you can always shop at your local department store and drugstore.

Building Your Makeup Kit

Here are some resources for starting your makeup kit, in a variety of price points:

- Alcone: www.alconeco.com

- Naimie's Beauty Center: www.naimies.com

- Sephora: www.sephora.com

- Ulta Beauty: www.ulta.com

- e.l.f: www.eyeslipsface.com

- Amazon: www.amazon.com

- MAC: www.maccosmetics.com

> The most important product may be desire—a willingness to attempt and explore the range of different looks made possible with makeup.
>
> —*Kevyn Aucoin*

Be Prepared: Essential Makeup Kit Items

You simply can't be a makeup artist without a full kit. You have to be prepared for every person you meet, and have colors and products in your kit to suit everyone. I also know it can be expensive putting all of this together, so I'll share my thoughts on which products you can save on and which ones you should splurge on. Here is a list of kit essentials:

- **Primer:** I can't stress enough how important this product is and why I can't live without it. Primer is just what it sounds like: a product to "prime" your canvas, the face. This product is usually clear and has a lot of "slip" to it, meaning it glides over the skin, preparing it for foundation and concealer. It fills in large pores, fine lines, smooths over dry, patchy areas, helps keep oil from breaking through, and keeps the makeup on longer. You'll minimize the need for your client to touch up, and the benefit to you as an artist is that you'll need less product to get an even, flawless finish. So now you know why I love it. Splurge on it. You can call and thank me later.

- **Foundations and tinted moisturizers:** You never know who you will meet in your work as a makeup artist, and you have to be prepared for every skin tone and skin type. Make sure to have a wide selection of shades available. The shades in my kit range from Porcelain to Espresso, with fourteen shades in between. You want to make sure to have sheer foundations and/or tinted moisturizers (my favorite), and a full-coverage foundation for those clients who may need a little extra coverage. This is definitely the biggest splurge item. I'd rather see you spend the most money here, because if the skin doesn't look perfect, then anything you do on top of it won't look good either.

- **Concealers/correctors:** Again, you'll need a range of concealers to match or coordinate with foundation shades. Make sure you have at the very least a light, medium dark, and a salmon or orange shade. I personally don't recommend buying "color correctors." They are essentially concealers that come in green, pink, and yellow to counteract redness, sallowness, or other skin pigmentation issues. It's been my experience that green concealer just makes you look green, and so forth. I'd rather see you invest in a few more shades of skin-toned concealers instead. Your concealer can also do double duty as an eye shadow primer, so, like foundation, it's a splurge; however, you'll save on purchasing a separate eye shadow primer.

- **Eye shadows:** You'll need a selection of matte and shimmer. To me, eyes are the most fun and make the most impact, so I'm constantly adding new shades to my collection. At the very least you should have a selection of neutrals in warm and cool shades; plums and eggplants, because they work on everyone; a navy, dark green, and a burgundy; and a selection of flesh-toned colors from ivory to a dark sand. This is a save . . . and a splurge! In my opinion, especially for novelty colors, you can find good shades and formulas in the drugstore or from lower-price-point lines. I would splurge on my core colors, the ones we talked about above, and save on the trendy, seasonal, or specialty colors.

- **Eyeliners—gel, pencil, or liquid:** To me there is only one choice when you're starting your kit, and it's gel liners. I would highly recommend starting with these. They can do double duty as a pencil or as a liquid liner, so they are perfect for the beginner. The benefits include the fact that they don't drag, and they have more pigment than a traditional pencil. You can create a defined line, thick or thin, depending on the brush. You can smudge them with shadow for a smoky look, or use them just as you would a standard liquid liner. This is a splurge, and can generally only be found in higher-priced lines, but you'll be saving in the long run because it's a double-duty product. Five or six good shades—a plum, black, brown, charcoal, and navy and/or green—will be all you ever need.

- **Mascara—waterproof and regular:** This is self-explanatory, and I would recommend just buying black (no brown, no colors). Black works on everyone, and let's be honest: Who needs navy eyelashes? This is also one product where you can save instead of splurging. In my opinion, there's no need to spend $30 or more on a mascara that will dry out and have to be tossed in a few months anyway. My all-time favorite mascara comes from the drugstore, so save your splurging for foundations and a few other key items.

- **Eyelash primer:** I love this stuff. Period. It lengthens and thickens lashes before you put the mascara on, and usually comes as a duo with the mascara. You can buy it at the drugstore so it's a save, and an economical way to plump up lashes without curling them.
- **Brow powders and pencils:** I prefer brow powders to brow pencils; in fact, I don't even have brow pencils in my kit. I feel brow powders look more natural and mimic natural hair better than pencils; however, you may choose which product works best for you. You'll need at least three to four shades: a light taupe for blondes and women with gray hair; a medium brown for blondes to brunettes; an auburn for redheads; and a black/brown for women with dark hair.
- **Powders:** You'll need setting powders and possibly foundation powders for your kit. I've found that mineral powders can act as both, depending on the brush you apply them with, so this is a good place to start. I prefer mineral powders that come in compacts, as the loose powders are very messy and can get on your clients' clothes. These are a splurge because they go hand in hand with foundation and concealer.
- **Blush—powder and crème:** When would I use a crème blush instead of a powder blush? Here's the general rule: Crème goes on top of crème, powder goes on top of powder. If you're using a crème or dewy foundation, you would use a crème blush. This works well for dry or mature skin. If you're using a matte or powder foundation, you would use a powder blush. And

Did You Know?

The women of the late Victorian era often made their own rouge, or blush, a concoction of strawberries, attar of roses, attar of neroli, deodorized spirit, pure carmine, and Russian isinglass (melted). The rouge was applied with a sponge. There were also commercial varieties of rouge available, often applied with a camel's-hair brush.

For women looking for a more natural alternative, beetroot juice could be applied with a camel's-hair brush.

here's a place where you can save; it's not necessary to buy expensive, top-of-the-line blush formulas.

- **Lipstick, lip stain, and gloss:** This is a category where you can save big. What's most important about the lips is the color. You can find reputable brands in the drugstore that carry a wide range of lipstick, lip stain, and lip gloss shades for every occasion. My favorite lip product is lip stain. It stays on longer than traditional lipstick formulas by leaving a "stain" of color on the lips. It's great for brides or events where your client may not have time to touch up. I like to layer the stain with a lipstick or gloss for extra pop and staying power.
- **Lip liners:** In my opinion, this product is optional and can be a money-saver. I personally use a lip liner only rarely, and that is usually if my client doesn't have a well-defined lip line (often the case with smokers, or with more-mature clients). I don't like the ring around the mouth they create, but this is your personal choice as an artist. I have a few on hand just in case, in a neutral flesh tone, a true red, and a deeper shade, like a rich plum.
- **Bronzer:** I have a love-hate relationship with bronzer. Some formulas can be too shimmery or too orange, so look for formulas that are matte and have some brown in them. I often use a mineral powder that is two shades darker than the client's skin tone. This can save you money if you already have some darker shades of powder in your kit.

So just to review, there are products we've discussed that you won't be able to live without. They solve a multitude of problems and will help you create smoother makeup applications that look more professional.

Did You Know?

In the 1920s, a woman could order the Armand Weekend Package, which included a face powder, rouge, cold cream, talcum, soap, and a booklet titled "The Creed of Beauty." The package cost 25 cents. For a dime, you could also order a sample of Pert, a waterproof rouge.

Makeup Kit Must-Haves and Have-Nots

These are your makeup kit must-haves:

- **Primer:** Smooths and evens out skin texture.

- **Tinted moisturizer:** A great alternative to foundation for most women.

- **Gel liner:** Long-wearing, easy to use, and versatile.

- **Lip stains:** Lots of staying power so they reduce touch-ups.

- **Mineral powders:** Can be used as foundation, setting powder, or bronzer.

On the other side of the coin, there are products on the market that in my opinion are a waste of money, because another must-have item can do double duty. As always, you can decide for yourself, but here are a few of my personal makeup kit have-nots:

- **Colored correctors:** Just avoid them.

- **Eye shadow primers:** Use your concealer instead.

- **Highlighter pens:** The average woman doesn't need these; use a shimmer eye shadow only in areas you want to highlight, even the cheeks.

- **Eye shadow duos or trios:** If you have some you love, that's fine, but invest instead in either professional palettes, where you pop pans of color in and out, or just buy individual shadows in exactly the shade you need. There's always one shade in a duo or trio that you won't use.

- **Gimmicky products:** Don't purchase things in cutesy, gimmicky packaging. Chances are you're paying more for the packaging than a similar product in plain packaging.

- **Beware of bronzers:** Steer clear of any bronzers that are too shimmery or orange.

Other Tools of the Trade

A makeup kit should be well stocked with a rainbow of colors, a paint for every canvas, but the tools you use to apply them are just as important. Makeup is painting, so think of it this way: It's the difference between finger painting and creating a masterpiece. You can't create a masterpiece without the right tools. Throw away those worthless applicators that come with the products when you purchase them. Brushes and the other tools you'll need in your kit may be an investment, but they're an absolute must.

- **Brushes and tools:** You can't paint a masterpiece without brushes. These tools of the trade are certainly a splurge, so invest in high-quality brushes. They may be made of natural hair or may be synthetic, depending on how you're using them. For the most part, for "dry" products (powder blush, eye shadow, setting powders, etc.), use natural hair brushes. For "wet" products, use synthetic brushes (foundation, concealers, cream shadows, or cream blush).

Brush Basics: What You'll Need to Get Started

Brush	Type	Used for:
Foundation brush	synthetic	liquid/cream products
Concealer brush	synthetic	liquid/cream products
Blush brush	natural hair	powder blushes
Eye shadow brush (large, fluffy)	natural hair	powder eye shadows
Eye shadow brush (small, fluffy)	natural hair	powder eye shadows
Eye shadow brush (small, dense, rounded)	natural hair	powder eye shadows
Thin eyeliner brush	natural or synthetic	gel or liquid liner
Slanted eyeliner brush	natural or synthetic	gel or powder liner
Eyebrow brush (slanted, stiff)	natural hair	brow powder
Eyebrow groomer	synthetic	brow grooming
Powder brush (large, fluffy)	natural hair	setting powder
Powder brush (large, fluffy)	natural hair	bronzer
Kabuki brush	natural hair	mineral powders

Note: You can add specialty brushes as you develop more techniques.

- **Brush roll:** Invest in a professional-looking brush roll to keep all of your brushes in. It looks organized, and helps you to easily find the brush or tool you are looking for.
- **Makeup case or rolling suitcase:** Most professional artists keep their products in a kit that's designed specifically for makeup artists, but they can often be pricey. If you're looking to save instead of splurge, consider using a suitcase. Whichever way you go, make sure that it rolls. You'll have a lot of product in there, and you don't want to have to carry a heavy bag each time you go out.
- **Cosmetic bags or resealable plastic bags:** Depending on the kit or suitcase you've chosen, you may want to separate your items into bags, by category. You can choose to splurge on clear cosmetic bags, which are great because they're durable, and you can see the products inside. The downside is they have to be cleaned regularly. The other option (and the way I carry my products) is resealable plastic bags. They are also clear so I can see the product inside, but when they start to look a little used, I just throw them away and put my product in new ones. The other benefit is, as your kit grows, there's more room to expand without buying pricey new cosmetic bags.
- **Tissues and cotton swabs:** These are essential for removing makeup, cleaning up around the eyes, and for blotting lipstick.
- **Disposable face wipes or cloths:** These are my lifeline. I use these for everything from cleaning up around the eye area before I apply concealer to cleaning my brushes in between application. I purchase them at the discount store for less than a dollar and keep them in stock. Be sure to look for the ones for sensitive skin.
- **Pencil sharpener:** Use for sharpening your lip or eye pencils.
- **Makeup remover—oil-based and water-based:** Makeup remover pads work well and are compact. You'll need a water-based remover for basic removal, but have some oil-based remover on hand as well, in case you have to remove waterproof products, like waterproof mascara or gel liners. If you opt for a jar or tube of remover instead of the pads, which is much more economical, you'll also want to purchase cotton cosmetic pads.
- **Moisturizer:** Have on hand a basic moisturizer that can be used on any skin type, even sensitive skin.

- **Eyelashes and glue (dark and clear):** It's important to have some basic lashes in your kit. These are perfect for brides and bridal parties. There are two kinds: strip lashes and individual lashes. They are both effective depending on the look you're going for, and the client's natural lashes. If your client already has moderately long and thick lashes, the individual lashes will work just fine. If your client has short or sparse-looking lashes, a natural strip lash is a better choice. With the lashes there are two types of glue to choose from, clear or dark. It's wise to have both, but if you want to choose just one, look for the dark. It has a dark tint so it's less visible as it's drying.
- **Manicure scissors:** These are handy for trimming or cutting eyelashes; they also come in handy when someone (like a bride) needs to remove a tag or a string from their clothing.
- **Tweezers:** Well-groomed brows will brighten everyone's face and help to frame the eyes. Tame unruly brows by tweezing any unwanted hairs. I also use the tweezers to help apply the eyelashes.
- **Bobby pins:** These serve double duty: They keep unwanted hair off of your client's face while you're applying the makeup, and I also use the tip of the bobby pin to apply glue to strip lashes and then press the strip into the natural lash line with the other end.
- **Disposable mascara wands:** For hygienic purposes, purchase disposable mascara wands so you can use a fresh one with each client.
- **Eyelash curler:** I don't use these often, but having one on hand is useful. Just beware of getting a "crimped" look. I only use these if a client has lashes that naturally grow straight out or down.
- **Visine:** Some clients may have bloodshot eyes or their eyes can be irritated by makeup, especially powder shadows. Have some Visine on hand to make sure their eyes are bright and clear.
- **Lip balm:** Keep some lip balm on hand to smooth out dry, chapped lips.
- **Hand sanitizer:** A small travel size of hand sanitizer is a great way to make sure your hands are clean, especially if you're working someplace where there may not be a sink handy.
- **Mints:** Because you are up close and personal with your client, make sure you have a tin of mints to keep your breath smelling fresh.

The following items are optional, but I can't tell you how many times they've come in handy for a bride or on a photo shoot. It's always nice when you can save the day.

- Safety pins
- Hair spray
- Deodorant
- Nail clipper and nail file
- Nail polish remover pads
- Hair ties or elastic bands
- Hair clips

When Should I Replace or Throw Away My Makeup or Clean Out My Kit?

Here are a few guidelines, but be sure to use your discretion. If a product is starting to look shabby, just go ahead and replace it. You want your kit to make a good presentation and always look clean and tidy.

- **Mascara:** Mascaras will need to be replaced the most often. You should replace them every two to three months, or when they start to dry out. Be sure to use disposable wands with every client to prevent risk of infection.

- **Eye pencils and eye shadows:** You can keep eye shadows and eye pencils for up to two years. You'll want to sharpen your pencils in between each use to keep them clean.

- **Lipstick and lip pencils:** These can keep for up to two years. Always use a lip brush to apply lipstick to your client, and not directly from the tube. You can clean the tip with wipes to keep the lipstick fresh. Lip pencils, like eye pencils, should be sharpened in between uses.

- **Blushes and powders:** Cream products should always be tossed before powder products. Your cream blushes should be kept about a year, while your powder blushes should be replaced roughly every two years.

- **Foundations and concealers:** A twelve-month shelf life applies to both oil-free foundations and concealers, which can dry out quickly.

Basically, when in doubt, throw it out!

Kit Hygiene Tips

Because you'll be working with so many people, you'll need to be very conscious of the cleanliness of your kit, the products in it, and your brushes and tools. A clean kit gives a client confidence that they're working with a professional. A dirty, junky-looking kit does just the opposite. Nobody wants to look like an amateur, or give their client unwanted germs. You won't win any friends or earn any repeat business by making people sick. Following basic hygiene tips will ensure that your client has a good experience and walks away healthy.

Keep Your Brushes Clean!

There's nothing more off-putting to a client than dirty brushes and tools. Make sure to clean your brushes in between clients. If you have several clients back to back in a day and don't have time to wash and dry your tools, use a sanitizing wipe or a spray cleaner and tissues to freshen them up. If you have time for them to dry, wash them in the sink with mild soap or shampoo and air-dry. Any synthetic brushes can be washed in between clients because they don't require drying time. In a pinch, and your natural-hair brushes aren't dry? Use a blow dryer to speed up the drying process.

Never Blow on Your Brushes

This is a big no-no. Blowing on your brushes is essentially just blowing germs onto the brush and then wiping them on your client's face. Instead, if you feel like you have excess product on your brush, tap the brush on the side of your finger or the side of your hand to release the product.

Don't Double-Dip Mascara or Lip Gloss

Use disposable wands for applying mascara and don't double-dip into the mascara with the same wand. If you need more mascara for the client, throw the wand away and use another one. These can be purchased at your local beauty-supply store. For lip glosses and lipsticks, use a clean lip brush. To apply lipstick, using the barrel of the lip brush, scrape a little of the lipstick off and apply it to a clean palette. I use the back of my hand as my palette, but you can also use a small painter's palette or tray instead. For glosses, first apply the gloss to the back of your hand or palette, then apply to the client. This is also helpful if you're mixing two colors to create a custom color for someone.

Always Wash Your Hands!

Make sure you keep your hands clean. Wash them in between each client, and if you're using the back of your hand as a palette, wipe the back of your hand and brushes frequently with antibacterial wipes. You can also keep a travel-size antibacterial hand sanitizer in your kit in case you can't get to a sink.

Create a Face Chart and Client Forms

Another key item you'll need is a face chart. Quite simply, it's an illustration of a face with sections for you to write instructions, colors, and products, so the client is able to take the information home and re-create the new look you just designed for her. It's basically a makeup cheat sheet for the client. The face chart is important, and can be used in several different ways.

One reason to use a face chart is to provide a take-home guide after a makeup lesson. The client then has a step-by-step face chart (kind of like paint-by-number) which includes the products and shades you used and instructions on how to re-create the look when she gets home. The chart is hers to keep and is a tool I know my clients rely on when practicing their new look. You may also want to make a duplicate of the face chart for your records so you have something to reference should your client call with questions about the techniques you used or the products you recommended.

The second reason you would use a face chart is to help you remember what you did for a bridal trial. For brides, it's important to have a chart of the colors you used because it may be six months or more from the time you did the trial to the day of the wedding. I don't know about you, but my memory isn't that good. I write down everything, from the size of the lashes to where I placed the eyeliner. The more detailed your notes, the easier it will be for you to recall the look you created for her, and the happier the bride will be with the results on the day of the wedding.

d. d. Nickel

Face

Pressed Foundation	$40.00	_____
Liquid Foundation	$40.00	_____
Sheer Tint	$40.00	_____
Oil-Blotting Powder	$32.00	_____
Retexturizing Face Primer	$40.00	_____
Concealer	$22.00	_____
Duo Bronzer	$32.00	_____

Eyes

Hi-Def Mascara	$23.00	_____
Lash Primer	$16.00	_____
Eye Pencils	$18.00	_____
Gel Liner	$20.00	_____
Eye Shadow	$20.00	_____
Brow Powder	$16.00	_____

Cheek

Blush (cream or powder)	$22.00	_____

Lips

Lip Liner	$18.00	_____
Liquid Lips	$20.00	_____
Gloss	$20.00	_____
Lipstick	$25.00	_____

Brushes and Tools

Deluxe Kabuki	$30.00	_____
Baby Buki	$18.00	_____
Ultimate Concealer	$22.00	_____
Total Face Coverage	$25.00	_____
Tapered Cheek	$20.00	_____
Lash Comb	$16.00	_____
Sharpener	$ 5.00	_____
Flat Shader	$16.00	_____
Thin Liner	$15.00	_____
Angle Blender	$16.00	_____
Large Blender	$16.00	_____
Wet/Dry Shadow	$15.00	_____
Cover/Fill In	$15.00	_____
Eyebrow Groomer	$15.00	_____
Under-eye/Lip	$15.00	_____
Brow Definer	$15.00	_____
Flat Liner	$16.00	_____
Moire Brush Pouch	$20.00	_____

This is the client card I use for my files and reference. This card reflects the shades, colors, and techniques I used on the client, but doesn't have the instructional face on the front (I no longer need the visual element of the face on the chart for reference).

Client Card

Date _____

Name _____

Address _____

E-mail _____

Phone _____

Current product selection/preferences:

_____

_____

_____

_____

Face

Pressed Foundation	$40.00	_____
Liquid Foundation	$40.00	_____
Sheer Tint	$40.00	_____
Oil-Blotting Powder	$32.00	_____
Retexturizing Face Primer	$40.00	_____
Concealer	$22.00	_____
Duo Bronzer	$32.00	_____

Eyes

Hi-Def Mascara	$23.00	_____
Lash Primer	$16.00	_____
Eye Pencils	$18.00	_____
Gel Liner	$20.00	_____
Eye Shadow	$20.00	_____
Brow Powder	$16.00	_____

Cheek

Blush (cream or powder)	$22.00	_____

Lips

Lip Liner	$18.00
Liquid Lips	$20.00
Gloss	$20.00
Lipstick	$22.00

Brushes and Tools

Deluxe Kabuki	$30.00
Baby Buki	$18.00
Ultimate Concealer	$22.00
Total Face Coverage	$25.00
Tapered Cheek	$20.00
Lash Comb	$16.00
Sharpener	$5.00
Flat Shader	$16.00
Thin Liner	$15.00
Angle Blender	$16.00
Large Blender	$16.00
Wet/Dry Shadow	$15.00
Cover/Fill-In	$16.00
Deluxe Spooly	$15.00
Under-eye/Lip	$15.00
Brow Definer	$15.00
Flat Liner	$16.00
Moire Brush Pouch	$20.00

Notes: _____

_____

_____

_____

_____

_____

_____

_____

_____

Tried-and-True Makeup Tips and Tricks

We've explored what you'll need in your kit to get started; now, how do you use some of these products, and what can you do to make sure your application is as professional-looking as possible? Following are a few easy tips and tricks to get you started.

Orange or Salmon Concealer

I told you that you needed it, but I didn't tell you why. Orange is the opposite of blue on the color wheel, which means that orange will counteract any bluish tones on the face. You'll find it particularly useful for someone who has dark circles under the eyes. If you try to conceal very dark circles with a light or medium shade of concealer, it will look ashen or gray, and will actually highlight the area rather than concealing or perfecting it. It's also great for covering bruises, and can even soften black eyes and small tattoos. You can use it on clients who have been tanning, and on even darker skin tones. So you see, it's a must in any kit.

White Eye Shadow

I use this to brighten the eye by placing a dot of the smallest amount on the tear duct of the eye. The bridge of the nose is where most women are shadowy and have darkness, so this helps to brighten the area in a subtle way.

Eyelashes

My personal preference when applying lashes is to cut one strip lash in half and use each half on the outer corner of each eye. It still looks natural if you choose the right lash product, and will give a nice sweep to the eye in photos. I also think they stay put

Did You Know?

Before the advent of false eyelashes, actresses, chorus girls, and performers used a technique called "beading" to enhance and extend their lashes. The tools necessary were eyelash beading makeup, usually black or brown, and a pan or spoon to melt it in. It was then applied to the lashes with an orange stick, or something similar. Each lash was painted separately so that a little bead hung on each tip. The technique apparently continued into the 1960s.

better than individual lashes. You can often find what they call "demi" lashes, which are essentially the same thing—they're just already cut for you. They're more expensive than doing it yourself. Another tip I have for you is not to splurge on expensive name-brand lashes unless you have a specific look you're creating that requires them. A good standard lash for bridal work and other events can be found in the drugstore. The most versatile and natural-looking lashes are #110 or #21.

Plum Is Good on Everyone!

I know we touched on this before, but it's important, especially if you're a beginner and not yet confident when it comes to choosing colors. When in doubt, a plum or eggplant (meaning deep, rich colors, not bright like purples) are universal and work well on all skin tones and eye colors.

Neutrals

Most women will tell me they like to wear browns or neutrals, and, to be honest, I think it's because they feel those shades are safe and they won't make a glaring mistake, which is completely understandable. No one wants to look like a lady of the evening, or worse, a circus clown, but my feeling is that *safe* doesn't create impact or "the wow factor." Introducing your client to color that's appropriate for her eyes and skin tone and showing her how to use it properly will go a long way toward creating a loyal client who trusts you. When choosing neutrals, try to avoid muddy or dull-looking colors and instead look for shades that have a red, plum, bronze, or gold undertone. These shades will still be in many clients' comfort zone, and will still give you enough color to highlight their features properly.

Should I Match What the Client Is Wearing?

The answer is no. I always consider what they are wearing, but I base my color choices on their skin tone and eye color more than what they have on. If your client happens to have bright blue eyes and is wearing a blue sweater, choosing a blue eye shadow would be total overkill. I would go with a brown or plum instead, to contrast with her eye color and create some balance. Remember, a color that contrasts with the eyes will make them pop. Sorry, folks—gone are the days of matching your makeup to your clothes.

Blush Placement

Not to sound preachy, but so many people are putting blush in all the wrong places. The technique that the majority of women are using (you know the one) is taking the powder brush and moving the blush back and forth from the hollow of the cheek all the way back to the hairline. Blush belongs only on the apples of the cheeks, just as its name suggests—only where you would naturally blush.

Contouring

Contouring is just creating shadow with a darker powder or foundation. There isn't any color involved at all. I would suggest not contouring unless you are working on a photo shoot or some other commercial project that may call for it. The amount of contouring that you would need to do to create different effects on someone would look garish on the average woman, especially during the day.

Bronzer

Where I use bronzer first is always on the neck. Our pesky chins seem to get in the way and shade our necks, so most women have color on their face and chest, and their neck is a little bit lighter. Start the bronzer on the neck where they need it most, and brush whatever is left over on the brush over the temples, forehead, chin, nose, and apples of the cheeks—anywhere the sun would naturally hit. Don't start the bronzer on the face. You'll have too much color where you don't need it, and not enough to warm up the neck. Remember, you can also use a powder two shades darker than the client's skin tone instead of a bronzer.

Trends

I'm a firm believer that your face isn't the best place to show your trendy side. Trends come and go in color and technique, and certainly, we all want to look stylish and up-to-date; however, I think the best approach to makeup is to always focus on your best feature and play that up with colors and techniques that work best for you. Let's face it: For the most part, our facial features don't change drastically from year to year, so if you've always had bright blue eyes or full lips, you should always play up that feature. My best advice is to interpret the trends without feeling like you have to participate in every one.

> The fact is, there is really no such thing as "normal"—
> everybody's different, and that is the essence of their beauty.
>
> —*Kevyn Aucoin*

Rookie Makeup Mistakes

Look, I've been there. I was a rookie once too, but the fact of the matter is, we all have to start somewhere. Making mistakes is a part of growing, so I'll share a few of my personal mistakes and the ones I see beginning artists struggling with. Keep the following suggestions in mind as you're practicing.

Identifying Skin Undertones

Warm versus cool. This can be tricky for the inexperienced artist because there are so many variations in skin tones, both light and dark. Warm skin tones are generally referred to as "olive," and cool undertones usually have a blue or rosy hue. To determine someone's undertone, look at the underside of their wrist where they haven't gotten any sun. Once you've determined whether they are warm or cool, it will be easier to choose colors that will harmonize with their coloring. Use colors with warm undertones to complement those with olive, tan, or warm skin tones. Choose colors with cool undertones to complement a client with a rosier complexion.

Too Much Makeup

The fact is, just because we're "artists" doesn't mean that we need to paint every last inch of someone's face. The idea behind makeup application is that we're highlighting someone's best features and minimizing others. If someone has beautiful, clear skin, you don't need to cake on the foundation. The best approach is to look at where there may be some redness or other slight blemishes and just use a tinted moisturizer, foundation, or concealer in those areas, leaving the rest of the skin clean. You should always take a step back before starting an application and recognize what you'd like to highlight and what needs to be perfected.

Too Much Highlighting

Without getting on a soapbox, this is one of my pet peeves. Again, too much of a good thing can be bad, and using too much shimmer or highlighting something that doesn't need to be highlighted is one of those things. Highlighting means just that: Wherever you put the product, that's where people will look. Most of your clients, if they're over the age of thirtysomething, will have a few fine lines or more, and using shimmer and highlight around those areas will just draw attention to them.

Matching Foundation Shades

This is a biggie. The stone cold truth is, if the skin doesn't look good and you haven't nailed the foundation color, then nothing you do on top of that will look good either. This is a deal breaker. Tinted moisturizers are good because they're sheer and a little more forgiving than traditional foundations, but either way, you need to know how to match foundation to your client's skin. Choose three shades to start with. Using a Q-tip, apply a generous swipe of each shade to the client's jawline. Let the shades sit for a moment and you'll start to see one shade disappear into the skin and the other two will start to stand out. The one that disappears is the correct shade. You'll also have to consider that many clients' face, neck, and chest will be slightly different in color; the neck may be lighter, the chest may be darker. You have to take into consideration both the chest and the neck when choosing the right shade so that when you look at the client from far away, her face, neck, and chest will match.

Color Choices

I watch rookie artists struggle with color choice all the time. The tendency for a new artist is to make everyone look exactly like she does because that is her comfort level. Just because you do a nice job applying makeup on yourself doesn't mean that you have the critical eye necessary to apply it properly on someone else. Makeup is meant to be fun, and certainly you should feel free to experiment, but most of your color choices should be guided by the rules of basic color theory. The chart on page 58 features a color wheel for your reference. Basic color theory states that complementary colors are opposite each other on the wheel. For example, blue is opposite orange, so they would be complementary colors; for you as a makeup artist, this means that these colors will make a client's features stand out. Again, these are guidelines, not rules, but as you begin to experiment and practice with color, you'll see how understanding the color wheel will work to your advantage and improve your artistry. As you read the following tips, keep the color guidelines in mind.

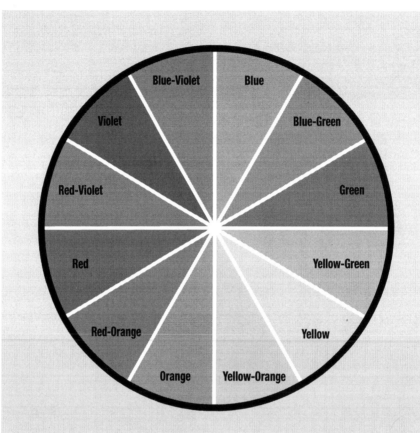

Color Suggestion Chart

Brown eyes	Navy, hunter or moss green, grape, teal, burgundy, charcoal
Hazel eyes	Burgundy, charcoal, soft gray, plum, gold
Blue eyes	Warm brown (orange or red undertone), plum, bronze
Green eyes	Eggplant, rich sable brown, burgundy, bronze

Here are a few of the basics:

- **Eyes:** When choosing eye shadow and liner for a client, you want to choose shades that contrast with their natural eye color in order to achieve the most impact. For brown eyes, using plums, navy, forest green, burgundy, and teal will provide the most definition. Can someone with brown eyes wear brown? Of course they can, but for the most impact, a contrasting color is best. If one of my clients prefers neutrals and has brown eyes, I'll look for a brown that has a plum or red undertone to it; grays can also be a nice option. For blue or green eyes, the same principles apply. Plums, purples, browns, burgundy, and bronzes are good choices. Blues, greens, and some grays, depending on the undertone, can be too close to their natural eye color. Notice that I mentioned plums for brown, green, and blue eyes. Because it contrasts with all eye colors, it's what I call a "universal" color. It works well on everyone, so make sure your kit has several shades of plum, eggplant, and grape.
- **Cheeks:** The best way to choose a blush color is to look at the color the client naturally blushes. Do they have a naturally cool, rosy undertone and blush in shades of rose or pink? Or do they have a warmer, bronzy complexion? In that case, you may choose a peach or melon color. Some clients are sallow and don't have much natural color in their skin. In that case, I choose a soft shade with just a hint of brown to it. A vibrant blush color would just look garish.

- **Lips:** Lipstick is one of the first cosmetics invented and still one of the most popular. It's an easy, affordable way to change your look. Again, the best choices are made when you've determined the client's undertone. Most lipsticks will a have a warm or cool undertone, so choose shades accordingly. And just like blush, take a look at the client's natural lip color. For the most natural, flattering look, choose a lipstick one or two shades up or down from her natural lip tone.

Putting on Concealer First

I'm going to save you a lot of hassle and cleanup by sharing this tip with you now: Most women, including new makeup artists, seem to start their makeup application by jumping in first with the concealer. This is wrong—and here's why. First, concealer is heavy and meant for full coverage. See what coverage you get by first applying foundation or a tinted moisturizer. Most of the time, this will be enough, and you may only need a little extra concealer around the nose for redness or to cover up a few blemishes. Whatever you do, don't conceal under the eyes until *after* you've applied the eye shadow. Any eye shadow that falls under or around the eye while you're applying it (trust me, this happens even to seasoned professionals) just makes it that much harder to clean up afterward. The eye shadow will stick to the concealer under the eye, be impossible to remove, and will actually accentuate any dark circles, defeating the purpose of concealing in the first place. Apply your eye shadow first, clean up under the eye with a disposable wipe or makeup remover, and apply concealer last.

Blush in All the Wrong Places

I've mentioned this pet peeve before, but it definitely bears repeating. Blush is meant to do just that—to mimic where someone would naturally blush, which is generally right on the apples of the cheeks. Blush was never meant to be back by the hairline or in the hollows of the cheeks. Those techniques were meant for contouring, which the average client doesn't need. So, beware of creating "stripes" of color on your client's face. Keep the color right on the apples.

Strong Lips and Strong Eyes

This is a biggie, and goes back to inexperience and the desire to enthusiastically over-paint someone's face. The face should always have balance. In order to achieve the right balance, you can choose to focus on one feature, either the eyes or the lips. I tend to favor the eyes because that's where I think you really want someone to look, but if your client has beautiful, lush lips, then making them the focus may be just the right thing. A dramatic, strong eye should always be paired with a soft, pale lip; likewise, a bold, vibrant, or deep lip should always accompany a soft, clean eye. If your client prefers a quieter look and isn't comfortable with either a strong eye or a bold lip, then create balance by using medium tones on both the lip and the eye. The bottom line is, having both strong eyes and strong lips can look garish and harsh on most women, so always take a step back when you are finished with the look and make sure you're happy with the balance you've achieved.

Being Afraid to Change Something

Nobody wants to be wrong or to look less than confident in front of a client, but I think the tendency for most new artists who struggle with an element of application is to leave the mistake instead of correcting it. The client will ultimately be happier with the look in the end if you go ahead and change something that may need to be changed instead of leaving her with a look she may be uncomfortable with.

> Glamour is not self-conscious; it's not trying really hard. It's just expressing your own truth. I think that's what the essence of glamour really is—expressing your uniqueness.
>
> —Kevyn Aucoin

Makeup 101: Technique Basics

You may or may not be a makeup rookie, but if you are guilty of making some of the rookie moves above, you're probably scratching your head and wondering how to move forward without making the same mistakes over and over again. You want to grow and learn but have no idea where to start. Here are some basic techniques that you can start practicing and experimenting with. The more you practice, the sooner you can start to build on these, tweaking them and making them your own. It's where we all start when we're learning. Find the techniques below that work best for you. Let's start with the Big Three: primer, foundation, and concealer.

- **Primer:** We've already discussed at length the virtues and benefits of primer. Just to review, it works wonders on everyone, and application is easy.

  Use your fingers to apply primer to the areas where there are large pores, fine lines, and dry patches.

  Depending on the primer and the amount of slip, a pea-size amount should be enough to cover the full face. If the client's skin is especially dry, you may need to apply more, concentrating it in the areas that are especially rough to the touch.

- **Foundation:** A flawless face is what every client wants and expects when she sits in your chair. Choosing the right shade of foundation is only half the battle. We've already discussed how to find that perfect shade, and hopefully you've been practicing that, but there are also some general application techniques you should follow to make sure the application is smooth and effortless. A flawless finish and perfect canvas should always be your goal.

  Apply foundation with a foundation brush, working only in downward strokes. Working in an upward motion disturbs fine facial hair, making it more noticeable.

  Start your foundation application in the center of the face and work outward and then upward. Apply foundation only where you need to even out the skin tone.

- **Concealer:** Almost everyone has areas that can benefit from concealer. Because it's heavier than foundation, you want to make sure you're only using concealer exactly where it's needed, most often on blemishes, red or blotchy areas, and under the eyes.

First, identify where you need concealer. Look for blemishes, redness (most likely around the nose and on the cheeks), and for any shadows under the eyes.

For blemishes and redness, apply concealer using a brush after you've applied foundation. Pat and blend the concealer into the area using your ring finger. If the concealer isn't a perfect match to the skin, mix it with a small amount of foundation that does match. Repeat this process until the area is well covered.

Around the eyes, start the concealer at the bridge of the nose. Most women are darkest here. Look for shadows underneath the eyes and cover with concealer using the brush. Pat any excess into the skin with your ring finger.

Clean up the outer corner of the eye using concealer. To find this line, place your brush at the ball of the nose and angle it out to the outer corner of the eye. The brush should meet the end of the eyebrow. This is the line you are cleaning up. This should remove any excess fallout from eye shadow or eyeliner, leaving the eye clean and open. On more mature clients, this technique actually gives the eye a "lift."

Eyes

They say the eyes are the windows to the soul, and in my opinion, it's the one feature that everyone should be highlighting. When someone is talking to you, you want them to look in your eyes. We'll look at a few techniques that focus on the peepers, but first I'm going to share with you a technique for eyes that will work on absolutely every eye shape, from round to almond and every shape in between. It works on every ethnicity and for every occasion. I use a variation of this technique on everyone from brides to celebrities, and it's the technique I teach in my studio during a makeup lesson. It's versatile and can be natural and fresh or smoky and sexy, depending on your color choices. You control the end result of the look with the intensity and depth that you apply.

Let's get started, step by step:

- **Prep and conceal:** The first step before any eye application is to prep the eyelids using a concealer from lash to brow. This will ensure that the color stays put all day long, and you won't have creasing or fading throughout the day.

- **Base color:** Choose a light, neutral eye shadow to use as a base color from lash to brow. You're just looking for a shade that will set the concealer and brighten the eyes a bit. Ivory, bone, tan, or taupe are all good choices depending on the complexion of your client. You want to choose a shade that mimics her natural skin tone.
- **Lid color:** Next, choose an eye shadow shade for the lids that adds some warmth or a pop of color. It should be a light to medium shade but have more impact than your base color. Apply the color to the lids from the lash line to the crease. Do not take the color above the crease. Rose, pink, peach, light browns, or more fashion-forward pastels or metallics will all work here.
- **Eyeliner:** Line the top lashes with a gel liner in a color that complements the client's eye color. Line all the way across the top lashes from the outer corner to the inner corner. (Note: I prefer gel liner to pencil or liquid liner. Gel liner goes on much smoother and doesn't drag like many pencils do or dry down as fast as liquid, making it the most versatile formula. It can be used for a well defined eye or a smudgy, smoky look.)
- **Accent color:** Choose a deep shade of eye shadow as an accent color for the lash line. Use a brush to smudge the gel liner with the darker eye shadow. Work right along the lash line, blending the shadow and liner together until it's soft and smudged, and there are no hard edges.
- **Define:** Use the darker shadow to create some depth and definition at the outer corner of the eye. Using a soft, fluffy brush, make a "V" shape at the outer corner of the eye, from the lash line into the crease. Blend all of the hard edges with a lighter shadow.

This technique works particularly well because all of the definition is along the lash line, which ensures that the focus is on the client's eyes, no matter what their eye shape is. Doing too much work in the crease or on the brow bone only highlights those areas. Keep in mind that where you put the most color and create the most definition or highlight is exactly where someone is going to look. We want people to look at the client's eyes, not their brow bone. "Wow, I love your crease color," or "Your brow bone looks especially shimmery today" are not compliments. Keeping all of the color and definition along the lash line brings the focus right where it belongs. As artists, it's our job to highlight the client's best features, and in my opinion, this almost always includes the eyes.

This basic technique has worked well for me in most situations, but if you have a client with a particular concern and you want to try some corrective work, or you're looking for a technique for a particular eye shape, here are a few suggestions for your beauty arsenal. Practice these so you'll be ready if you have a situation that calls for them.

Close-Set Eyes

Your goal with close-set eyes is to create the illusion of width, making them seem farther apart. To create width, you want to keep the inner corners light and create more width and definition at the outer corners.

- Start by prepping the eyelid with concealer and a light, neutral shadow, as above. Use a light shimmery shadow on the very inner corner. This is where the brightest highlight color should be. Extend this color to the center of the lid.
- Next, apply a light to medium shade on the center of the lid, right above the iris of the eye. Use the deepest shade of eye shadow in the outer corner, from lash line to crease. Blend all three shades together so there are no hard edges.
- Line the eyes by applying liner across the lash line from the outer corner to the inner corner. To widen the eyes, keep the liner at the outer corner thicker and make it thinner as you move toward the inner corner. For smaller eyes, line only the top lash line.
- Create some sweep at the outer corner of the eye with extra mascara.
- Make sure the brows are well groomed. Clean up brow growth close to the nose and extend the ends to help open up the eyes.

Wide-Set Eyes

If you feel the clients eyes are wide-set, you can create an illusion of closeness by reversing the steps above and using the darker shade at the inner corner, making the shadow lighter as you work toward the outer corner.

- Start by prepping the eyelid with concealer and a light, neutral shadow, as above. Use the lightest shadow on the very outer corner. Extend this color to the center of the lid.
- Next, apply a medium shade on the center of the lid, right above the iris of the eye. Use the deepest shade of eye shadow in the inner corner from lash line to crease. Blend all three shades together so there are no hard edges.

- Line the eyes by applying liner across the top lash line from the outer corner to the inner corner. For smaller eyes, line only the top lash line.
- Create some drama with mascara across the top lashes.
- Make sure the brows are well groomed and not too thin. Keeping the brow growth closer to the nose will help to give the illusion the eyes are closer together.

Prominent Eyes

Prominent eyes are set forward in the face and are the most prominent feature. Using light shades will only highlight the prominence of the eyes. Darker shades across the lash line and on the lid will help minimize and correct.

- Start by prepping the eyelid with concealer and a light, neutral shadow, as above.
- Apply a dark eye shadow over the entire lid and extend the eye shadow into the crease but not up into the brow bone.
- Line the eyes using a deep, rich eyeliner from inner corner to outer corner. A thick line, either well defined or smudged, is appropriate for prominent eyes.
- Use a highlighter just under the brow to lighten and lift the eye.
- Apply plenty of mascara to emphasize the top of the lashes.

Small Eyes

If the client's eyes appear small, start by prepping the eyelid with concealer and a light, neutral shadow, as above.

- Apply the lightest shadow on the eyelids.
- Apply a soft, medium shadow in the crease.
- To brighten and open up the eyes, apply a highlighting shade under the brow.
- For a more mature client, use a matte highlighter.
- Next, line the upper lash line with an eyeliner that's not too deep or dark.
- Apply black mascara on the upper lashes.

Hooded Eyes

If your client has hooded eyes, you won't be able to see their eyelids when they look straight ahead or their eyes are open. You'll want to brighten up the lids and warm up the brow bone. You'll see this type of eye most often on mature clients.

- Start by prepping the eyelid with concealer and a light, neutral shadow, as above.
- Apply the lightest shadow on the lid.
- Apply a medium or dark shadow at the outer corner.
- Line the upper lash line with a liner that can be smudged. Avoid harsh, well-defined lines. An alternative is to line with an eye shadow for a softer look.
- To warm up the brow bone, have the client look straight ahead and locate the orbital bone. The orbital bone is located right above the crease of the eye. On the outer half of the orbital bone, apply a pop of blush, bronzer, or a warm shadow that coordinates with the rest of the look. Because this area is what will be most visible, you'll want it to look blended and soft but still be accented.
- Apply black mascara to upper lashes.

Deep-Set Eyes

You can recognize deep-set eyes when the crease of the eye is very deep and defined and the orbital bone and brow may be more prominent. To even out the contrast and brighten up deep-set eyes:

- Start by prepping the eyelid with concealer and a light, neutral shadow, as above.
- Apply a light, shimmery shadow across the lids to help brighten them.
- Apply a medium or dark shadow along the orbital bone and blend it down and into the crease. You want to be sure not to make the crease too dark, which will make it recede even more. Focus most of the color along the orbital bone.
- Use eyeliner across the upper lash line for definition.
- Use mascara on top lashes only.

Asian Eyes

For Asian eyes, it's best to graduate the color, using the darkest shade along the lash line and working up and out toward the brow bone.

- Start by prepping the eyelid with concealer and a light, neutral shadow, as above. Start with the darkest shadow along the lid, using it at the outer half of the eye and extending it up and out at the outer corner.

- Start blending the darkest shadow with a medium shadow. Move the color up toward the orbital bone at the outer half of the eye. The inner corner should still be light, with most of the color concentrated at the outer half of the eye.
- Use the lightest shade to blend up into the brow bone, starting at the inner corner and working the color diagonally toward the outer corner of the eye.
- Line the top lash line, keeping the line tight in the inner corner and thicker toward the outer corner.
- Curl and build lashes using lash primer and mascara.

Did You Know?

Any eye shadow can instantly be turned into an eyeliner by wetting a liner brush with water, or a product called eyeliner sealant. This is a great alternative for more mature clients, or for anyone who would benefit from a softer, more natural approach.

Lashes

There will be many times—particularly if you're working on brides or you're putting together looks for your portfolio—that you'll want to use false eyelashes. They can be intimidating if you're new to makeup artistry, but having the right techniques will make the process much smoother. You'll need tweezers, lashes, lash glue, manicure scissors, a bobby pin, and a steady hand for these techniques.

Individual Lashes

- First, remove a lash from the tray with tweezers.
- Place a small amount of glue on the back of your hand and dip the end of the lash in the glue.
- With the client's eyes closed, place the first individual lash at the outer corner of the top lash line. Press the lash as close to the natural lashes as possible with the end of a bobby pin.
- Repeat the process until you've reached the desired look. I recommend using at least a minimum of three individual lashes on each eye, placing them from the outer corner to the middle of the eye.

Mascara

Mascara is another one of the application techniques that can make a newbie artist sweat. Not only are you working closely to the delicate part of a client's eye with a sharp wand, but many clients also have a tendency to blink, which can make applying the mascara that much more difficult.

- To begin, have the client look directly over your shoulder. With their eyes looking over your shoulder, ask them to look halfway down.

- With their eyes cast halfway down, you can apply the mascara to the top and the bottom of the lashes efficiently.

- Using your mascara wand, start at the base on the underside of the lashes and wiggle the brush back and forth to build up volume at the lash line. Then, pull the wand up the full length of the lashes to create length.

- Use whatever product is left on the wand to coat the topside of the lashes from above.

- If your client is blinking, make sure that they aren't looking directly into a light source. That can often be the problem.

- If your client is still blinking and you're having trouble safely applying the mascara, have them cast their eye downward as before and hold the wand steady near their lashes. Have them blink directly onto the mascara wand.

- You can also bend the brush perpendicular to the wand to create an "L" shape. Bending the brush can make it easier to get into the base of the lashes because the angle is easier to work with.

- Place lashes close together for a thicker look.
- Individual lashes come in different lengths. Use the longer lengths at the outer corner and the shorter lengths as you move in toward the inner corner.

Strip Lashes

- Pull the strip lash from the tray using the tweezers.

- Line the lash up against the client's eye line and decide where to trim the lashes. Many strip lashes are too long for the client's eye shape and need to be trimmed to fit accordingly.
- Place a small amount of glue on the back of your hand.
- Take a bobby pin and open it up until it is one length. Dip one end of the opened bobby pin into the glue.
- Using the end of the bobby pin, apply the glue to the edge of the strip lash all the way across.
- Place the sweep of the strip lash along the outer lash line using the tweezers. Align the rest of the strip lash along the lash line until it is lined up where you would like it.
- Using the clean end of the bobby pin, start pushing the strip lashes down as far as you can get them into the natural lash line. Work from the outer corner to the inner corner until the lash is secure.
- Every once in a while, the lashes will stick to the bottom lashes. Have the client look up in between each lash application to make sure the top lashes aren't sticking to the bottom lashes from the glue. In the event the lashes are stuck, gently release the lashes using the clean end of the bobby pin. To eliminate this problem, use as little glue as possible.

Brows

Even the best makeup job on eyes won't look as good without a well-groomed brow. Brows frame the eyes and can make the eyes look more open with the right shaping. You may or may not be professionally shaping brows for your clients, but even some simple tweezing to get rid of strays and filling in the brows with brow powder where needed can actually change the look of someone's face.

- To determine the best shape for someone's brows, use the end of a long makeup brush. (You can also use a pencil.)
- To find the beginning of the brow, place the brush along the ball of the nose and up to the brow. Where the brush lands is where the brow should start. If there are hairs on the nose side of the brush, remove them with tweezers.
- To find the arch, keep the brush on the ball of the nose and move it to the outside part of the iris of the eye (the part of the iris closest to the outer

corner). This point should be the highest point of the arch. Remove any stray hairs below this area to open up the brow.

- To find the best place for the brow to end, keep the brush on the ball of the nose and rotate it toward the very outer corner of the eye. Where the brush lands is where the brow should end.

- Once you've determined the shape and cleaned up the brow, take a step back and look to see if there are any sparse areas. Using a brow powder in a color that matches your client's natural brow color, fill in just the areas where there are holes. Brush the brows with a brow brush to blend the powder into the hair.

- If the brow stops short at the end, extend the brow using the brow powder and blend out with a brush.

Hopefully you're now feeling confident that you can master a few eye techniques, but no look is complete without cheeks and lips. Let's take a look at some techniques to make sure your finished look is polished and clean.

Cheeks

We've already touched on the fact that blush should be applied just where someone would naturally blush, not in the hollows of the cheeks. To make sure you're putting the blush right where it belongs, follow these simple steps:

- Have your client smile. Locate the roundest, fullest part of their cheek, called the "apple."
- Place your brush right on the apple of the cheek and blend the color back toward the hairline.
- Be sure not to get the blush too close to the eyes, which will close up the features. To ensure proper placement, lay your index finger along the side of the eye, between the outer corner and the top of the cheekbone. The blush should never go above this space where the finger is.
- As you blend the color back toward the hairline and temple, be sure the color starts to fade where the eyebrow ends. You don't want full color on the hairline or the temple. Remember, these areas would never blush on their own, so there should be little color there.

Lips

Believe it or not, lips can be tricky, and they are one of the hardest things to get right—especially if you're doing anything more than a sheer gloss. Try this technique:

- If you're using a lip liner, use the side of the lip liner, not the tip or the point, and start to "color" in the lips, just like you would in a coloring book. Start in the center of the lips and work out to the edges.
- Apply lip color on top of the lip liner using the same technique with a lip brush. If you're not using a lip liner, start the technique with the following step instead.
- To ensure the lip line is clean, use a small amount of concealer on the side, not the tip, of a concealer brush. Place the brush with the concealer just underneath the natural lip line. The brush should rest on the natural shape of the lip. Drag the brush along the line to clean up any mistakes. Do this on the top and bottom lip line until the edges are clean and precise.

05

Setting Prices

As fun as being a makeup artist is, and as many times as I've happily done someone's makeup for free, just for sport, or to feed the creative giant inside, you just can't make a living at it if you're not charging what your time and skills are worth. The million-dollar question is: How much should you charge, and how do you go about quantifying what your time and talent are worth? We'll look at several things you'll need to consider when you're putting together your menu of services and rates. The first step is determining what sets you apart from the other artists in your area.

Determine What Sets You Apart

Why should a potential client pick you? What makes you special and sets you apart from the rest? Are you known for your natural approach to beauty, or are you known for a more glamorous look? Are you an expert at choosing colors and products or great at enhancing a particular feature, like the eyes? Make a list of your strengths as an artist and use that to find your area of expertise. Not all artists have the same strengths or vision, and your client will be attracted to you for what makes you special. I brought with me years of experience and a background as a seasoned makeup artist. My clients are attracted to my level of skill and expertise in the beauty industry. They're looking for real answers to their lifelong beauty challenges, and an experience that goes beyond department-store makeover or tips found in beauty magazines. Determine your strengths, decide what sets you apart, and capitalize on that.

I also find that clients will choose you as their makeup artist when they are able to relate to you as a person. If you're a fresh-faced twentysomething, chances are, the client that will be attracted to you will also be a twentysomething. If you're a mom of two, then other moms will also be able to relate to

Check the items that best apply to your strengths and skill as a makeup artist.

Personality

❏ I'm comfortable meeting new people.

❏ I have a friendly, outgoing personality.

❏ I am open-minded.

❏ I'm a good listener.

❏ I enjoy working a flexible schedule.

❏ I enjoy making people feel good.

❏ I'm a helpful person.

❏ I like being around people.

Artistry

❏ I consider myself an artist.

❏ My favorite subject in school was art.

❏ I have a good eye for color.

❏ I enjoy studying and reading about fashion and entertainment.

❏ I have always done makeup for my friends and family.

❏ I enjoy painting, drawing, crafts, or other artistic pursuits.

❏ I love experimenting with color.

❏ When I'm shopping, I always come home with new makeup.

❏ I have years of experience working in cosmetics.

❏ I'm good at explaining how to apply makeup.

❏ I experiment with different makeup looks regularly.

❏ When I look at someone, I can immediately see what makeup would enhance their features.

❏ I understand the laws of color theory.

Explain briefly why you are interested in becoming a makeup artist. What has drawn you to this field?

_____

_____

_____

you. It's not a hard-and-fast rule, but I think people will be attracted to you not just based on your personality and artistry skills, but because they feel you'll be able to understand their particular beauty needs and challenges. Women want to feel beautiful at every age, and they're looking for someone who understands them and whose opinion they can trust.

Shopping Your Competitors

You won't know how to determine your services and set your prices if you don't know who your competition is, what they offer, and what their prices are. Get out there and do some research, either on the Internet or in person, and find out who your competition is. What services are they offering? Do they have a spa or salon, or are they independent artists who travel to the client? What are their rates? What is their niche or area of expertise? Are they catering to the bridal market or to the mom on the go? Once you've seen what others are doing, you can decide where you fit in.

The Internet is the best place to start your search. Searching for websites of people in your immediate area is the best place to begin, since these artists will be your direct competition, but don't limit your search to just your particular area. You may be inspired or find a unique approach from an artist in another part of the country that appeals to you. A simple Google search is the best place to start gathering information. If the artists in your immediate area have a storefront, studio, or work out of a salon, you may consider stopping by or setting up a time to meet. Some artists may be open to answering your questions about their makeup business and the industry in general.

Shopping your competition is certainly an important step in determining where you'll fit in, and it's also important that you continue this practice long after you're established. I still check every week to see if there are new artists or if anyone is offering new services. I like to see how the competition is marketing themselves, if there are any rate changes, and if there's anything new happening in my area. Make this a part of your routine and you'll always be able to keep a fresh perspective on your business.

Determining Your Services

When I first started on this adventure, my only intention was to offer makeup lessons. I put together a customized lesson that I thought addressed all of the needs of my intended client. I knew she had disposable income. I knew she was most likely thirty or older, possibly with children, possibly with a career, but either way, she'd spent her life confused, going from store to store, counter to counter, magazine to magazine, looking for real answers to her unique beauty concerns. She was tired of being accosted in the department store and didn't know where else to turn. She would be willing to pay to have a professional answer her specific questions and give her real advice. As people started to hear about me, I had requests for other services that I've added along the way. They all address different needs and events in a woman's life. Based on your area and your intended clientele, determine which services work best for you and how you'd like to customize and tailor them to your business. Some of the most common services include:

- **Makeup lessons:** Teaching someone how to choose colors that are appropriate for her and how to apply them. Everyone's instructional and teaching style is different, so decide how long you will spend with each client and what items you'll cover in the lesson. If you've never done a lesson before, ask your friends or family members to be your first, and walk through the lesson with them. Ask for their feedback and what they would like to learn. Time yourself so you can let the client know what to expect.
- **Makeup applications for special events:** This could be a makeup application for a girls' night out, a gala, attending a wedding or bar mitzvah—essentially any special event that may come up where a woman wants to look her best.
- **Makeup parties:** In-home makeup parties have become popular, just like parties for jewelry and kitchenware. If you are aligned with a line of makeup to sell, then this is a good way to introduce a large group of women to your products all at once. If you don't sell makeup, this is still a fun night and a way to introduce yourself and your services to a new set of faces. You may want to offer tips, do a demonstration on a model, or conduct one-on-one mini makeovers on each participant.
- **Seminars and workshops:** You can create a desire for your services by offering group workshops or seminars where you can demonstrate product and technique. You can approach women's groups and organizations, and even corporations.
- **Children's and teen parties:** Offer your services to young girls for birthday parties or a group of teens just learning how to do their makeup.
- **Bridal services:** Makeup for the bride and her bridal party. You can even consider offering makeup parties to the bride and her friends for a fun bachelorette night out.

Pricing Your Services

Pricing your services accordingly can be make or break for your business, so it's important to carefully assess how much you'll charge for each service. There are standard rates within each market, and your pricing should be within a reasonable range of what others are charging. You don't want to price yourself so high that no one can afford you, and you don't want to price yourself so low that clients will question the quality of your work. The bottom line is, you need to strike a balance between what people will pay and what your time and skill is worth. Your pricing should always reflect your level of experience, training, and what is appropriate for the market in your area.

I struggled with this in the beginning. I tried to strike a balance between what I thought women in my area would pay for makeup lessons and what my time was worth. I landed on a figure that works for me. Would I get more clients if I lowered my rates? Quite possibly—but probably not the type of client who would appreciate my expertise and experience. Would I like to charge more for my services? Of course, but I also believe that there is only so much a woman is willing to pay for a makeover, especially when she can get one for free at the makeup counter.

I think it's also crucial when you're pricing your services to be realistic about your skill level. As an example, maybe the most experienced and established artist in your area is charging $100 for a makeup lesson. If you have less experience, you shouldn't expect people to pay the same amount for your services. Because makeup artistry is a skill and a service, not a product, you need to set your rates accordingly. You'll have greater initial success and build a suitable clientele for your skill level. As your confidence and business grows, you can expect to adjust your rates.

Offering Discounts, Special Promotions, and Extras

Now that you've determined what your competitors are offering and you've nailed down your services and rates, what can you do to offer a little something extra? Is it in the experience you provide? Do you have a technique or look that is unique to your area? Do you offer a new service or have a different perspective on makeup application? Finding ways to offer your clients extra services or reasons to visit you ensures loyalty and repeat clients. Some of these suggestions will work for your particular client base, and some may not. Let's take a look at some possibilities and how they may or may not work for you.

Offering discounts typically means offering a percentage off the price of your services or products. I think the effectiveness of discounting is based on what motivates your client. If your client is a high-end one, with plenty of disposable income, she may not be driven to take advantage of your services just because there is a discount. However, if your client is a budget-conscious working mom, even a modest discount may be just the incentive she needs to call you and book an appointment. I personally have tried discounting my services and found that it doesn't work for me; my client just doesn't seem to be driven by that. She'll come and see me when she's ready and in need of some help. For me, providing a traditional discount card or offer just hasn't worked. With that said, I know other small business owners who have had great success discounting their rates at certain times of the year, or for special events. Having a clear snapshot of your client's profile will help you determine whether discounting will work for you.

You may find instead that special promotions are more effective for you. This can include anything that encourages the client to either book you for the first time or for a return visit. Instead of offering my client a discount on my services, I often give her a new product or color to try. Everyone likes a gift. Many of the big beauty companies offer what they call a "gift with purchase," a gift bag of free sample-size products the client receives for making a full-price purchase. If you don't sell product, you could run a promotion offering a free makeup service to anyone who sends you a referral, or a "bring a friend" promotion: two makeovers for the price of one. The options are endless, and can change as your business grows.

Offering extra services is another way to keep traffic moving in your direction. Do you have other skills that you can offer to your client? Have you had training or are you knowledgeable in skin care? Skin care and makeup go hand in hand, and many women will look to you for advice on both. Can you expertly shape brows? Brows frame the eyes and can make or break the eye look you've created. Being skilled in waxing, threading, or tweezing brows will only enhance your skills as a makeup artist. Have you been trained in eyelash extensions or eyelash tinting? Any other related beauty service that you can add to your menu will always add to your business. See chapter 12 for more information on how to expand your business through extra services or selling retail.

06 Branding Yourself

As silly as this may sound, as makeup artists, we're not reinventing the wheel. Many before us have been successful makeup artists, and many more will follow us. Makeup has been around for centuries, so what is it that will make you special? What is it about your personal philosophy and makeup style that will set you apart from the rest? You have to think long and hard about what qualities you possess as an artist that will attract people to you. These are the qualities that will define you as an artist and will start to shape you and your talents as a brand.

Defining Your Style as an Artist

Every artist has a personal makeup style. If you're new to makeup, you may still be experimenting to find your voice, but it's in there, and the more practice and experiences you have, the more your style will develop. Even if you're not yet sure of your personal style, you may find yourself attracted to a particular type of makeup or certain looks that you see on others or in magazines. Some artists find their strength is a natural, effortless look, while others prefer more glamorous makeup. Some may lean toward vintage or pinup looks. There are so many styles and techniques of makeup, and you need to know what it is that sets you apart before you can attract the right client. It all goes back to determining who your client is, what her needs are, and where you fit in. Developing your sense of style is crucial in branding yourself and attracting the right clients.

What if you like all types of makeup? That's great, actually; so do I. There's no need to limit yourself. A great artist is able to be flexible, creating different looks for different situations. I've worked on projects from Broadway to runways, and all of those experiences in between have required my creativity, but I still have a signature style and a philosophy surrounding makeup, one that resonates with my clients. For example, I like a well-defined eye, soft cheeks, and a medium to nude lip. I've created techniques along the way that work for me. I have a voice and something to share with my clients that goes above and beyond what they've learned in the past or read in myriad beauty magazines. My strength is beauty makeup, and the techniques I use work for every woman.

Also consider that part of branding yourself and defining yourself as an artist goes beyond the type of makeup you do. Your appearance should also reflect your signature style and look. If you're wearing strong, dramatic makeup, women looking for a natural touch will probably be hesitant to book your services. The opposite can be true: If you wear almost no makeup, those looking for a dramatic look may search for someone else. There are no hard-and-fast rules here. The point is, style yourself to highlight your personality, reflect your personal makeup style, and define yourself as an artist. Women will be attracted to you and trust you to guide them if they like the way you present yourself.

Choosing a Name and Logo

Every business needs a name and a logo. You need to be recognized by both, so it's important to choose something that reflects your particular business and your personal style. Your name and logo may be one of the first impressions you give to a client, especially if they find you online or through another form of marketing. You need to ask, "What does my logo and business name say about me?"

I knew right away that I wanted to use my name as my business name. My experience and résumé is what sets me apart and defines me as an artist, so using my name was important to me; however, my full name was too long and just sounded too wordy. I chose to use my nickname instead. It's what my grandparents always called me, so it has special meaning, and it also has a nice ring to it. You may want to use your name too, but if part of your plan is to manage a group or team of artists, you may want to consider using a name that speaks to the type of makeup or services you will offer as a group.

Now that you've chosen a business name, you'll need a logo. But how do you go about creating one? If you're like me, you're not a graphic designer. There are actually many options, some of them free, believe it or not. Depending on your budget and how much you can invest, there are a variety of options. Let's take a look at the free options first.

A simple Google search of "create a logo" will pull up many websites offering free logo design. These sites offer very basic icon, text, and color choices, and although you are somewhat limited in design, they are free, and you can create a very effective, simple logo in less than five minutes. Many of the sites will then give you the option of ordering business cards and other marketing materials on the spot, featuring your new logo. It couldn't be easier.

Another online option is a site that gives you access to graphic designers who will create a logo based on your requirements. A great website, called www.99designs.com, allows you to hold a competition. Graphic artists compete to create a logo for you based on the information you provide, and you can then choose the one you love and that speaks most to your business. The rate starts at $295, so it's more of an investment, but you get a custom logo at a fair price. You can also take a look at www.logomojo.com. Their customized services start at $195, and you can work one on one with their group of designers.

If you're at all handy with Photoshop or another photo-editing program, you can purchase illustrations and photos to use for your logo at www.istockphoto.com. I created my logo using an illustration from this site, and my brother customized it for me using Photoshop. You can purchase the illustration for use at a very reasonable price, so if you're computer-savvy, this may be an economical option for you.

If you're on a budget and would like to work with someone directly, search for graphic design students who may need a project to help build their portfolio, or who would like to make a little extra money. Many graphic artists need material for their portfolio, so seeking out someone interested in your project in exchange for using your logo to promote their work is a win-win for both of you. You can place an ad on Craigslist, or find graphic design students through your local college or art school.

And of course, if you want to make a big splash and you have a budget, you could work with an already-established graphic designer. Be sure to ask for client referrals and to see a portfolio of work before getting started. Be clear about what you like and what you don't like, and be sure you have some direction for your logo before you meet.

Designing Marketing Materials

Just like creating your logo, there are many ways to create striking, effective marketing materials. Depending on your budget, there are a variety of resources in different price ranges to help you put together the materials you'll need to sell and promote yourself.

Business Cards

The first and most important marketing material you'll need is a business card. This is an important tool, so I suggest creating the best card you can within your budget. People will keep your card if they are interested in booking an appointment with you, so you want it to be durable and to make a lasting impression. I had a client who recently booked a makeup lesson with me. She'd kept my card in her wallet for three years until she was ready to finally book her appointment.

The best online resources I've found for creating business cards are www.vista print.com and www.overnightprints.com. Their prices are reasonable, and you can create your own card online. If you can afford it, have your cards printed on heavier stock so they are more durable, and if your logo has color in it, print the cards in full color so they are more eye-catching. If you'd like to work with someone directly instead of designing the cards yourself, online, you can visit your local print shop where someone can help customize a card for you.

Business Card Sample

front

back

www.ddnickel.com   dd@ddnickel.com
203.777.4161   917.400.1721 cell

Other important marketing tools are postcards and brochures. I've found that sometimes I need something larger and more memorable than a small business card. I've used brochures and postcards at events that include many other vendors, and where my small business card may get lost in the shuffle or drown in a goodie bag of vendor information. I've found them useful at bridal shows, expos, women's events, and makeup parties. I have them outside my studio so prospective clients can take one as they walk by, and I send them to other businesses, like photographers, to pass along to their clients.

Your postcard should be colorful, reflect the style of your business, and include your logo and contact information. I always include a photo of my recent work on my cards to keep them looking fresh and interesting. Postcards are also a great place to put any offers or promotions you are running, like a free bridal trial, or a percentage off your services. My resources for postcards and brochures are the same as my business cards, but you can do a Google search for "create postcards online" and a number of services will pop up. Browse until you find postcard and brochure designs with templates and prices that work for you. See examples of my promotional materials on pages 85 and 86 for inspiration.

Putting Together a Portfolio

If I could offer only one piece of advice to new artists, it would be this: Put together a strong portfolio. You're a makeup artist. People want to see your work. They say a picture is worth a thousand words, and in this case, it's true. Every makeup artist, no matter her client base, needs one. Simply put, a portfolio is a collection of photos that show your work. I can't stress enough that this is one of the most important steps you can take in starting your business as a makeup artist. A strong portfolio will sell your services long before the client even contacts you, and will help you stand out from your competition. It's one of the first impressions you'll make on potential clients, and one of the first things they'll judge you on. If they like what they see, they will call and inquire further about your services. If they don't, they'll move on to the next artist.

When I first got into makeup artistry, portfolios were primarily hardback, leather books with prints of your latest work in them. Because of our fast-paced, technology-driven world, a hardback book isn't a necessity anymore, but can still be a valuable marketing tool when you're meeting with a client. However, your portfolio should

front

d.d.Nickel
~makeup~

Celebrity Looks for Real Women

back

Makeup~Customized Lessons~Bridal Services~Special Events

www.ddnickel.com~ 203.777.4161~by appointment
Visit me at www.styleconfessions.com for makeup tips and tutorials

Learn. Paint. Create

d.d. Nickel

makeup studio

front

Runways, Red Carpets and a Broadway Stage...

Celebrity Makeup Artist, d.d. Nickel, has more than a decade of experience making faces look radiant for the camera. She matches her talent and love of color to every client's individual needs and personal taste.

Products

d.d. Nickel signature line of makeup

Services

One-on-One Lessons
Bar/Bat Mitzvahs
Special Occasions
Makeup Parties
Bridal

Visit

ddnickel.com

By Appointment
203.777.4161

inside

always be accessible online and constantly updated with your newest and best work. Make sure to incorporate your work into your website as galleries, and separate the galleries by category. If you have a lot of bridal work, create a "bridal gallery." If you have photos of non-bridal work, like headshots, family portraits, or beauty shots, also separate these into categories. You'll want to separate your work so that it can be viewed quickly by clients browsing your site.

Your portfolio should be diverse and show that you can work with a variety of people. By this I don't necessarily mean that you need to have everything from bridal to avant-garde looks. In fact, when I look at a website and there are too many different types of makeup, I think it can be confusing to the client. What I mean by "diverse" is a range of ages, ethnicities, and styles—something for every potential client to relate to. For example, if your business is focused on bridal work, there's no reason to have a photo in your portfolio of a "rainbow" inspired eye. Brides don't want rainbows on their eyes for the big day, so keep your portfolio relevant to your client. Clients should be able to relate to your portfolio and sense your signature style when they view your work.

Does creating a portfolio sound like a big undertaking? Well, it is—and it takes a certain time commitment, but doing it right will drive the business you're looking for straight to your door. So where do you start? If you don't have any photos of your work, then recruit family and friends to be your models. Do their makeup and take their photos with the best lighting and camera you can find. You can even do "before" and "after" shots to show off your makeup skills. Snapshots of friends and family aren't ideal for a portfolio, but it's a good place to start if you don't have any photos at all. Be critical of your work. If you don't love the makeup or the photo, then don't use it. It's better to show no work in the beginning than to show work you're not happy with.

Once you've gotten your feet wet and you have a few shots of your work, contact local photographers or photography students and set up test shoots of your work. In the industry, they call it "testing," among other terms (see "Industry Terms" on page 88). In short, it means that the photographer, model, makeup artist, and anyone else involved in the shoot can use the photos provided by the photographer for their own portfolios. There is no money exchanged; it's just a day of shooting so everyone can have quality photos of their work. It benefits everyone involved, so don't be shy about contacting photographers you admire via e-mail or a phone call. Ask if they would be interested in setting up a test shoot. In my experience, most photographers are open, especially if it's their off season or they have some downtime. For example, if you're looking to test with a wedding photographer, they are often available during the week because most weddings are booked on the weekends.

And of course, you'll also need models. Certainly, you can ask friends and family, but if you want more diversity in your portfolio, you may need to look elsewhere for willing faces. Your city may have local modeling and commercial talent agencies. Many of their aspiring models and actresses also need photos for their portfolios, so they may be willing participants, especially if they are also new to the industry and trying to build their portfolios.

There are also online sites for those aspiring to get into the modeling and photography industry. These sites are resources for all of the talent needed to put together a photo shoot, including makeup artists, so you may consider adding your profile to the site so others can find you as well. My only warning is to make sure you ask a lot of questions before booking any sessions off of any of these sites. Make sure the work they are presenting online matches the style you want for your portfolio, and ask to see their professional website or portfolio in advance. The site most widely used is www.modelmayhem.com. It's part social media, part booking service. You can connect and make friends with new models, photographers, and more, just like you would on Facebook, but you can also create casting calls and send e-mails directly to the talent you'd like to work with.

Another benefit to putting together photo shoots with local photographers, hair stylists, and models is networking. Meeting like-minded, creative professionals who work in the industry is a great way to build your business. Most photographers work in a variety of genres, including headshots, family portraits, engagement sessions, weddings, and much more. That leaves a lot of opportunity for a makeup artist. When a photographer likes your work, they are more likely to call you or recommend your services the next time they need someone to do makeup.

There is also a growing trend in the wedding industry called "styled shoots." This means that a group of wedding vendors get together to coordinate a mock wedding, using the images for their portfolios. We'll talk more in depth about the benefits of styled shoots later, but participating in these shoots will provide you with the same basic benefits: quality photos for your portfolio, and networking opportunities.

Creating a Website and Blog

Now, unless you've been living under a rock, you know that everything that happens these days is in cyberspace. Gone are the days when people would look to the phone book to find service providers. The Internet is where everyone gets information and finds services, including makeup artists. In today's marketplace, having a strong website is an absolute must, not merely a suggestion. In fact, a recent study revealed that only about 11 percent of households actually pick up a phone book to find services these days. That means roughly 90 percent are using the Internet as their main source of information. Today, your website is your first impression. A potential client will decide how they feel about you and your services based on the presentation of your website. The more dynamic and well-put-together it is, the better the impression. Your website should reflect your personality, showcase your work, and be visually appealing to the style of client you're trying to attract.

As a makeup artist there are a number of things that must be on your site. Your site should include the following categories:

- **Biography:** Those visiting your website will want to know about your background, including your interest and experience in the makeup artistry field, along with any related education and training. While it's important to keep your biography relevant to makeup artistry, you should also infuse some of your personality into it. Nobody wants to read a dry, stale story of your entire life history. Keep it relevant, light, and fun. It's also a good idea to include a photo of yourself—the more professional, the better. People want to see who they are making an appointment with.

- **Portfolio:** Because you are a makeup artist and it's a visual art, there must be photos of your work. I recommend organizing them into galleries so clients can quickly locate the type of makeup services they are looking for.
- **A listing of your services:** Create a page listing the services you offer.
- **Contact page:** This page should include your phone number and e-mail address. If you have a studio space or storefront, you should also include your physical address and a map and/or driving directions.

You may also consider:

- **Listing your rates:** Some artists list their rates, others do not. This is a personal choice and may be determined by your market and your price range. Clients all have different budgets, so if you feel your client is driven by cost, I would recommend posting your rates. If you have a high-end clientele, listing your rates may not be necessary.
- **A list of your current clients or résumé:** If you've had extensive experience and have a list of impressive clientele that you think will appeal to your client, then certainly include this on your site.
- **"Before" and "after" photos:** Many women are impressed when they see the transformation that can happen with successful makeup application. "Before" and "after" photos are a good way to showcase your work and your ability to change someone's look.
- **Links to your preferred vendors or other beauty professionals, including hair stylists, manicurists, and wedding vendors:** A referral, even online, is a powerful tool. If you admire the work of another artist or business, let your clients know. Maybe they'll do the same for you.
- **Links to your favorite sources for purchasing makeup:** Recommend places for your clients to shop for makeup if you are not selling a particular brand.

Add a Blog

What is a blog? Well, I can tell you, outside of building my website, it's been one of the most effective marketing tools and one of the best decisions I've ever made in promoting myself. We'll talk more about self-promotion and online marketing later, but for now, a blog is simply an online diary or journal of your work, or you can think of it as your own personal online newsletter or magazine. Clients can even subscribe to your blog, just like they would subscribe to a magazine, which will send your blog posts directly into their e-mail in-box.

You can blog or write about anything you'd like, really, but makeup-related topics are the most obvious. The idea behind a blog is that your potential client can get to know you before you even meet. It's what will make them feel comfortable with you. With a blog, they can hear from you regularly, keep up with your current work, make comments, and feel connected. It's the tool that will help you attract the right clients. I don't know how many times I've met a client for the first time and have them say they felt they already knew me just by reading and following my blog. When you're choosing what to write about, keep in mind that your blog topics should match the audience you're writing for. This comes back to who you are as an artist, what makes you stand out from the rest, and why a client should be interested in your work over that of another artist. Focus your blog topics on what you know best, and remember—your blog is an extension of your personality. While you want to keep the posts relevant to makeup, don't be afraid to infuse them with other things that are happening in your life. You'll want to share those things that you would share with someone in person if you were just getting to know them.

The more technical aspect of why a blog is important is the fact that your website is static—meaning, the client doesn't interact with your site. Your website is

Blog Topics

Here are just a few suggested topics you can blog about that are makeup-related:

- Seasonal makeup tips and trends

- A creative photo shoot you collaborated on

- Your favorite makeup looks and how to achieve them

- New makeup products you recommend

- Online videos and tutorials

- Behind-the-scenes photos of you working at a wedding or photo shoot

- Any affiliations you might have or places where you donate your time doing makeup (like Look Good . . . Feel Better or Dress for Success)

essentially your online business card and your introduction to the client, while your blog is a way for someone to get to know and connect with you. It's the difference between meeting someone new at a party and shaking hands or actually having a conversation. You're more likely to connect with someone once you've had a chance to really talk.

Make sure your blog is connected and accessible through your website. You want clients to be able to read your blog directly from your website. Your blog should look as similar as possible to your website so both will appear fully integrated. It should include your business name, logo, and any taglines you'd like to include.

There is another benefit to having a blog. In many cases, your blog will come up more readily in search engines than your website, meaning that if someone is searching for a makeup artist in your area, they may see your blog before they see your website. Your blog allows you to "tag" each post, meaning at the end of the post, you would include words that are relevant to that post. For example, if you write a blog post about your favorite new mascara, your tags may look something like this:

Tags: mascara, makeup artist, best new product

Your "tags" are the words that someone would type into a search engine when they are searching for a new product or service. The tags allow the search engine to match your post with the query. You can choose any keywords you think are relevant to the post.

So how do you get started? There are many sites out there that offer free to low-cost blogging platforms. I've included the most popular platforms with their pros and cons.

Blogger.com

This is one of the easiest blogs to set up and is ideal for the beginning blogger. If you just want to get your feet wet without any commitment, this is a good place to start. It's easy to set up, easy to use, and it's free. You don't need any content (meaning already-written material) to get started. It's also remotely hosted, which for you means there's no extra charge for a domain name or a hosting account. The downside is it's difficult to customize it on your own, and in my opinion, without customization, it looks less professional than other blog platforms. It's a basic blog and a good place to start. This is where I started, but I quickly realized I needed to upgrade.

Wordpress.com

Wordpress.com is a good option for the beginner or intermediate blogger. It's still relatively easy to set up, moderately easy to use, and free. It has more templates to choose from than Blogger.com, and can be more easily customized to integrate with the look of your website. No content to minimal content is needed to get started (this depends on the template that you choose). It's also remotely hosted, so there's no need to have a domain name or hosting account. Another upside is that if you started with Blogger.com, you can export your previous blog posts to Wordpress .com, so you won't lose any of your content when you upgrade. If you think blogging is something you'd like to incorporate into your website, I would recommend starting with Wordpress.com.

Wordpress.org

This platform is definitely for a more advanced blogger. There are countless templates and designs to choose from, most of which require a significant amount of content. If you've been blogging for a while and have plenty of content, you may look into upgrading to Wordpress.org. It's self-hosted, so you'll need a hosting account and a domain name, which you may already have, depending on your website. It is very customizable and there are a lot of ways to enhance your blog with what are called plug-ins. The downside is it's more difficult to set up on your own, although I was able to do it by myself with some research online. Many of the templates resemble actual websites or even e-zines (online magazines), so their presentation is more impressive and can be much more visual.

Whichever way you decide to go, be sure to add photos to all of your blog posts. Remember, you're a makeup artist. Potential clients don't just want to hear from you, they want to see your work.

Marketing

To be honest, before I started this adventure, I had no idea what "marketing" really entailed. I had no need to market myself before I opened my business, and never even gave the concept a second thought. It was just a subject somebody else studied in school, one of those boring cubicle jobs for some other poor schmuck. Boy, was I wrong. I now know why people graduate with degrees in it and create entire careers around it. It's time-consuming, creative, and rewarding when you get results. It can take up more of your time than actually doing makeup, but it's a must. You really don't have a choice. The only real choice you have is *how* you market yourself, and that's what this chapter is all about. The bottom line is, you need to market yourself, or no one is going to know who you are or where to find you.

Introducing Yourself and Creating Awareness

So how do you spread the word? I wondered the same thing when I was getting started. How would I let everyone know that I was available to do makeup? The first step I took was to compile a list of other small businesses that might already be servicing my intended client. Targeting already-established businesses instead of individuals just makes good sense. It's easier to market yourself to other business owners, and you'll reach your target market sooner. The other upside is networking with other savvy business owners. In my experience, other small business owners are typically very supportive and open to helping each other out.

You can choose to contact other small businesses any way you think is suitable. You can call, send an e-mail, or visit their places of business to introduce yourself. I chose to send out a promotional kit introducing myself and my services. They were handmade and reflected the style of my studio and website.

I wanted to send out something that looked special and wouldn't automatically be overlooked or thrown directly in the trash, so I styled my kits to look like an invitation. I sent these kits to every local business I could think of that provided services to women.

In addition, I also sent out promotional kits to newspapers, local magazines, and TV shows. You can even send kits to friends, family, and coworkers that may be interested in your new services.

My promotional kits included my logo, biography, client list, services, and contact page—just like my website—and directed them to my site for more information. I made them myself using card stock and ribbon from the local craft store, but you can also have something put together professionally if you're not the crafty type. What's important is that it reflects your personality and lets people know that you're open for business.

Another option to consider is creating an e-mail campaign, a powerful and instant tool, and free. I put together a professional-looking e-mail and searched the Internet for the wedding vendors in my area that I thought had a similar aesthetic to mine, possibly sharing the same type of client. I e-mailed each of them and introduced myself. This resulted in some immediate connections, a few of which came to fruition later on. Either way, the result was positive. It created awareness, and I made some quality contacts with some fantastic vendors.

Another idea is to host an opening party or create an event. If you're not opening a storefront, consider renting a space or hosting a party with another small business

How to Create E-mail Campaigns

Two great websites for creating e-mail campaigns and newsletters once you've made some contacts are www.mailchimp.com or www.constantcontact.com. Your web hosting company may also offer an e-mail service. These services offer templates for making professional-looking e-mails, and offer the client the option to unsubscribe if they don't care to hear from you. One word of warning: Be careful of spamming. These services have very strict policies about spamming, which means sending unsolicited e-mails. I would only use these services once you've made some initial contacts and have an e-mail database of people interested in hearing from you.

owner, perhaps a local hair salon, designer, or day spa. Ask other small business owners to join you for the promotion. Perhaps a caterer or wine shop would be willing to supply the food and wine. Invite a florist or event planner to decorate the space, or a local boutique to put together a fashion show. I think every small business understands the value of cross-promotion, and many are willing to participate. Invite the local media and have everyone invite their client lists. If you're not that ambitious, consider just hosting a girls' night out for friends, family, and coworkers. Ask them to invite women they know who might be interested in your services. Do mini makeovers or a demo on one of the guests so everyone can see your work. Word of mouth is powerful, so anyone you touch that night may be the one to send you your next client.

Create a Strong Online Presence

There's simply no replacement for the power of the Internet. If you have a strong presence online, it will make it significantly easier to get your business moving in the right direction. One of the most important elements is search engines, the biggest and most powerful being Google. There are others, including Yahoo and Bing, but Google is the one that will drive the most potential business to your website.

Gone are the days of the Yellow Pages. Outside of word of mouth, you need search engines because that's how most of your clients will find you. Today's Google is yesterday's phone book. There are several ways to get the word out about your business, but first we need to explore SEO, or Search Engine Optimization. For our purposes, SEO simply means that your website or blog will come up first when a potential client is searching for makeup artists. Most people when searching for services will only look at the first page of results, so you want to ensure you have a presence there. Google estimates that it processes over a billion search requests daily worldwide from users looking for desired goods, services, and products. That's a lot of opportunity for your website to get noticed, and you want to make sure your site is the one that gets noticed first.

When you're creating your website, experts recommend you include some key elements to make sure your website comes up in searches. Google offers a free SEO Starter Guide that will walk you through the steps needed to create a search-engine-friendly website (http://static.googleusercontent.com/external_content/untrusted_dlcp/www.google.com/en/us/webmasters/docs/search-engine-optimization-starter-guide.pdf).

Google Places

Another tool for ensuring placement is called Google Places. It's a listing that comes up among other local listings at the top of the first Google page. It's a place for you to list your services, hours of operation, address, contact information, reviews, and more. You could consider it a mini Google web page that will direct people to your more-comprehensive site. It's inexpensive and offers a lot of bang for the buck. This is a great option if your services are more localized. There is no monthly contract, and you can cancel the listing at any time. There is a monthly fee, but it's minimal compared to other forms of advertising. To find out more about listing and rates, visit www.google.com/places/.

Here is a screenshot of how your Google Places listing will look after someone has done their search.

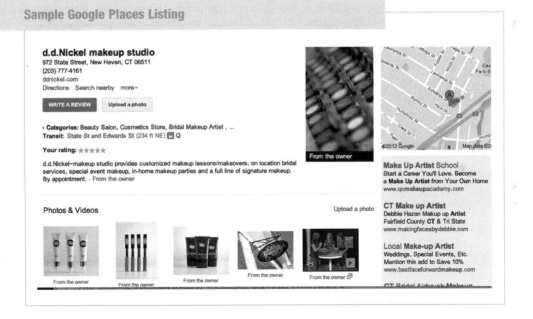

Sample Google Places Listing

Google AdWords

Another option is called Google AdWords. If you do a Google search and see listings to the right of the page, or highlighted ads at the top of the page, those are Google AdWords. These types of ads are called pay-per-click, or "sponsored ads," which means you only pay for the ad when someone clicks on it. These ads connect people directly to your website. You set the budget for your ad each month, and can control where the ad will be seen by choosing keywords that people may use to find you. This is also an inexpensive way to advertise compared to traditional print advertising. Google will also place your sponsored ad on other relevant sites, like bridal or fashion websites, for extra exposure. Like Google Places, there is no contract, and the ads can be canceled at any time. You can learn more at www .adwords.google.com.

Here's an example of how your Google AdWords listing will look:

Celebrity Makeup Artist

In-Studio and On-Location Makeup

Lessons, Bridal Services, Events

www.ddnickel.com

And here is how it will look in the search engine. The Google AdWords are to the right of the screen, and the Google Places listings are to the left, marked by a red indicator.

Sample Google AdWords Listing

d.d.Nickel makeup studio
www.ddnickel.com/
Located in New Haven, **Connecticut**, the **studio** offers **make up** services and signature products ...
Place page

(A) 972 State Street
New Haven, CT
(203) 777-4161

Allure Hair Studio
www.myspace.com/allurecoventry
3 Google reviews

(B) 3 Mason Street
Coventry, CT
(860) 742-4444

Bridal Hair & Makeup Studio
www.gorgeousbrideny.com/
Home | About us | Your Big Day | Services | Our Portfolio | Bridal Expo | Press | Contact us ...
1 Google review

(C) 95 East Putnam Avenue
Greenwich, CT
(203) 561-2164

More results near **Connecticut** »

Makeup Artist Connecticut
atouchofcolormakeup.com/
A Touch of Color Make-up is a full service **makeup artist** specializing in Wedding Make-up in **Connecticut**, airbrush make up, airbrush tanning, make up academy ...

Makeup Artist Training Connecticut - Make Up Artist Schools ...
atouchofcolormakeup.com/academyclasses.htm
Location: A Touch of Color **Make-up Studio** llc. 194 Leavenworth Rd. Suite I 2nd Floor Rt 110 White Hills Shopping Center Shelton **Ct**. Pre Requisites: None ...

Connecticut Wedding **Makeup Artists** and Beauty
www.weddingreports.com/**connecticut_wedding_makeup_beauty**.cfm
Find the best wedding **makeup artists** in CT along with other **Connecticut** beauty ...
Airbrush Makeup & Hair by Naomi's **Studio** & Salon, West Hartford, (860) 232- ...

Map for **connecticut makeup artist studios**

in **CT**-look your absolute best-

Famous Artists in CT
www.ctforum.org/creative-minds
Lyle Lovett, Dave Eggers & More!
Get Tickets for Unique Event Here.

See your ad here »

Google Places versus Google AdWords

Here's a comparison between Google Places and Google AdWords:

	Places	AdWords
Free	Yes	No
No website required	Yes	No
Pay only for clicks	N/A	Yes
Monthly budget control	N/A	Yes
Daily budget control	N/A	Yes
Ads on Google Search and Maps	N/A	Yes
Ads on Google Mobile Search and Mobile Maps	N/A	Yes
Ads on Google partner sites	N/A	Yes
Multiple ad formats: Display and YouTube	N/A	Yes
Ability to target ads geographically	Local	Anywhere

If you're just starting your business, I would recommend investing in both of these and seeing which one works best for you.

Another way to show up in a Google search is a blog (see chapter 6 for more details about creating a blog). Your blog posts often show up in search engines before your website does. When I Google any number of keywords, it is always my blog that shows up first.

Online Directories and Outside Links

These create links back to your website. In the beginning, I signed up for as many affordable sites as I could find. Now that I've gotten the word out and my site comes up on the first page, I've cut back, but here are a few suggestions of sites to consider.

- **www.weddingwire.com:** This site is powered by Martha Stewart, and the best thing about it is, it's free! You can create a gallery of your work, connect with other vendors, and invite clients to review your work. The categories for review are: Quality of Service, Responsiveness, Professionalism, Value, and Flexibility. There is also an option for you to respond to reviews. Having positive reviews online is a selling point for many clients, so this site can be a particularly useful tool.

- **www.yelp.com:** This is also an online review site, specifically for services. While WeddingWire is targeted to potential brides, Yelp is more general, so this is a good place to get reviews from those who have used your makeup services for other reasons, like makeup lessons.

Some other sites you might be interested in include:

- www.theknot.com
- www.brides.com
- www.partypop.com
- www.betterfly.com
- www.thumbtack.com

Traditional Marketing versus Online Marketing

There's a reason that marketing and advertising is its own specific career field. Figuring out the best way to advertise and market yourself will take up as much time, if not more, than actually doing makeup. There are so many options out there, and it's hard to know where you'll get the best results. Without sounding trite, it's simply trial and error. You'll try something once and if it doesn't work, then you'll try something else. The options these days are endless, some of them traditional and some of them nontraditional.

Traditional Marketing

Traditional marketing includes placing ads in newspapers, magazines, and other publications, or advertising on television, billboards, or through other media outlets, like radio. If you have an unlimited budget, then some of these options may be right for you. I've tried a number of things over the years, and have found traditional advertising to be very expensive without much result. I do believe these avenues work for many types of businesses, just not makeup artistry. If you do choose to place ads, be sure that your ad is reaching your target audience. Find publications and programming that are specifically geared to your client, like a bridal or women's beauty magazine. The more targeted your audience, the better return you'll have on your investment. In my opinion, there are other ways to reach people without spending a lot of money, and that's online.

Online Marketing

Online marketing includes advertising on blogs, being active on social media sites like Facebook and Twitter, and getting links on other blogs and vendor websites. Let's take a look at blogs first.

Blogging has suddenly become one of the most powerful tools for advertisers. Even big corporations have taken notice and are now spending a portion of their advertising budgets on blogs. Because of a blog's reach, it's also a powerful tool for you. Blogs have essentially become the new magazine or newspaper, and the benefit is, they are numerous and generally very targeted. Advertising on the right blog means you reach the right client. Some blogs will have areas specifically designated for paid advertisers, and the fees are usually very reasonable. Seek out blogs that appeal to you and that you believe would appeal to your type of client. Take note of the other businesses advertising with them. Do their businesses seem like a match with yours? That's usually a good indicator that your client is their audience. Also frequent the blog to see if the same businesses are advertising regularly, which may be a good indication that they are getting results. Paid advertising on specific blogs is a great way to start advertising with a smaller budget.

Here are some blogs you may want to check out for inspiration, and to see what advertising options are out there.

- www.stylemepretty.com
- www.weddingchicks.com

Some blogs, in addition to offering paid blocks of advertising, also have paid links to preferred vendors. Searching blogs in your area that offer advertising space is certainly worth investigating and investing in.

There are other ways to get exposure on blogs without paying for advertising, and a few of those are free. One of those is called *guest-blogging*. Not all blogs will have an area for paid advertising, but all blogs need regular content. The blog editor may not be the only one doing the writing, or may not have time to do all of the writing. To run a successful blog you need to post new content several times a week, if not more. If you find a blog that you particularly love and connect with, and think it would also be a blog your potential clients might be interested in, approach the creator of the blog with some possible post ideas that would benefit both of you. Keep in mind that the blogs don't necessarily have to focus on makeup or beauty. They can be any blog that attracts women, including topics like fitness, health, fashion, or parenting. Remember:

Any post you put out there into cyberspace will live there indefinitely, so the more posts you produce, the greater the chance that new clients will find you.

Another way to get exposure is to have a link to your site on other websites or blogs. Many other small businesses and wedding vendors will have links on their websites and blogs of other businesses they recommend. I have links on the sites of photographers, hair stylists, aestheticians, and other businesses I've connected with over the years. You may consider having a place reserved on your site for links to businesses you recommend.

And one of the best ways to connect and spread the word, for free, is through social media sites. The two most used are Facebook and Twitter. If you're not already on social media sites, I highly recommend you start. These sites are the new version of the best way to build your business: old-fashioned networking. It's just networking in cyberspace rather than a physical space. The top dog in social media at the moment is Facebook, and there are several ways you can use it to make yourself known. First, there is your personal page, which many of you may already have, but you can also create a page specifically for your makeup business. You may also want to check out Twitter, another good social media platform. All social media sites have their niche, and we'll delve deeper into their differences, how to use them to your advantage, and how to get started later in chapter 8, but for now, consider these social media sites a must for successful marketing.

Investing in Bridal Shows and Women's Expos

Bridal shows and women's expos are just another way to gain exposure in your area, and to a very targeted audience. Let's start with bridal shows.

Bridal shows usually happen twice a year or more, depending on your market, and are targeted to brides who are planning their weddings. The shows are usually hosted in a wedding venue or larger arena, depending on the size of the show, but they all feature every vendor a bride would need to plan her wedding day. For you as a vendor, that means exposure to potential brides interested in booking a makeup artist. There is generally a fee to be a vendor at a bridal show. The rates can often be pricey, so it's important to weigh the pros and cons before making the investment. You'll also need to have marketing materials on hand to distribute to potential brides, and display materials to decorate your station and sell yourself, so keep those costs in mind when making a decision. You'll also need to be sure that the company who is running the show is marketing it to your type of bride. Investing in a show and not getting any return is a big risk.

Keep in mind: Not all events are created equal. My first two bridal shows were a total bust. There was money going out and no money coming back in. I spent hours putting together a slide show, bought some audio/visual equipment, and made postcards and brochures. I did my best to put together an attractive, eye-catching display, and spent hours greeting bride after bride. And after all of that, I didn't book a single bride, or receive any inquiries, for that matter. And why was that? The bottom line is, they just weren't my brides. The company marketing the bridal show attracted brides that quite simply didn't have the budget to include a makeup artist in their big day, at least not one with my rates. So, do your homework. The organizers should be able to give you some statistics on the average budget of the bride they are attracting and what services they tend to book. You should even ask for a list of past participants and get their feedback before committing.

Another opportunity may be women's expos. With a quick Google search you may be able to find some in your area. The idea behind them is the same as a bridal show. There are a collection of vendors and activities that appeal to women, all under one roof. There may be a fashion show, shopping at vendor boutiques, beauty services, and more. Think of it as a girls' night out, only bigger. The obvious advantage to participating in an expo is the opportunity to meet a lot of women and hand out your marketing materials. You may even want to bring your makeup kit and chair and offer mini makeovers or touch-ups. Again, just like the bridal show, make sure the event is targeted to women who would actually be interested in your services. In this case, ask the organizers for the median income of the women attending, what services have been popular, and for a list of vendors that have participated in the past.

Creative Marketing Alternatives

Because makeup artistry is creative, there are also many others ways to market yourself that don't follow the traditional business models. We talked at length about building your portfolio and how to get started. One of the best ways to not only create beautiful images for your portfolio, blog, and website, but also to get some exposure through social media, blogs, and other websites, is to participate in "styled photo shoots." What? Aren't all photo shoots styled? Yes, in some ways, but we're talking about creating a photo shoot that's specifically intended for publication purposes and based around a need in the marketplace, not just to add pretty pictures to your portfolio. The goal is increased exposure.

Styled Photo Shoots

Styled photo shoots are very popular in the bridal industry and are popping up across the country, particularly on bridal blogs. A group of wedding vendors will get together and collaborate on what is essentially a "mock wedding." The creative end of a project like this is the freedom to come up with a storyboard and make it a reality in photos. The practical side of a styled shoot is that you get to collaborate with other vendors, which creates new relationships and working partnerships. The marketing benefit is these shoots can be submitted to high-traffic, targeted blogs where they may be published, just like a magazine. Your best work, published, means more exposure and in the end, more clients. Creativity, networking, and marketing, all combined in an afternoon of fun. What's not to like about that?

The other great thing is, you can initiate it. Don't be afraid to approach other vendors with your ideas and see if you can put together a team to produce a styled shoot. Collaborate with a wedding planner, florist, wedding designer or boutique, and photographer to bring your vision to life. Then submit the image per your desired blog's guidelines. If the blog editor wants to publish your images, then presto, good work! Mission accomplished. If the images aren't published, then remember the other valuable benefits of a project like this: You still have beautiful images to use for your site and marketing materials; you've formed new relationships with quality vendors; and you've enjoyed the freedom to be creative. It's a win either way.

To see what published shoots look like, visit the inspirational blog, Style Me Pretty, at www.stylemepretty.com.

Donations

Donating your time or services is another way to gain exposure and make the world a better place at the same time. If you have a favorite charity or organization that you support, ask how your services might benefit them. Perhaps it's donating a gift certificate for a silent auction, event, or fund-raiser. If you don't already have a charity that you support, you may want to get involved in one, or join other organizations that support women and their needs.

Here are a couple of well-known national organizations that may interest you, and where your services might be needed:

- Look Good . . . Feel Better: www.lookgoodfeelbetter.org
- Dress for Success: www.dressforsuccess.org

Getting Press

Everybody loves a little press, and they say any press is good press, no matter what kind it is. Celebrities thrive on it, and some even build careers on it. It's the good, the bad, and the ugly, and we buy into it, hook, line, and sinker. I thought long and hard about how I could get some free exposure and the answer was press. I didn't have an advertising budget, so *free* was what I could afford, and the best idea I could come up with. My first little bit of press came through a local newspaper. A friend of mine knew the entertainment reporter and recommended she put a small mention about me in one of her columns. Presto! Six appointments just from that one mention in the newspaper! Now that's what I'm talking about. Free press.

So with that in mind, I tried to come up with other ways to connect with the local media. I sent press kits introducing myself to the local bridal magazines. Several months later came an inquiry. Would I be interested in giving a quote for an article they were writing on bridal beauty? Of course! Another score. Two weddings booked because the brides read the article and liked what I had to say.

And then there was television. Honestly, who doesn't want to be on television, at least once? Although I'd worked behind the scenes on many sets, I didn't have much on-camera experience. However, when you're starting a new adventure, you really have nothing to lose. I contacted the local television station by e-mailing the news anchor, and to my surprise, she e-mailed me right back, asking me to do a beauty segment for their noon news. Gosh, that was easy! My point here is, don't be afraid to reach out to your local media. They need content and stories as much as you need the exposure, and you never know where one article or one on-air segment will take you. That one TV segment on the noon news has led to regular appearances doing beauty segments for the station.

So, how do you get a little press for yourself without all of the usual Hollywood antics and the hefty price tag of a publicist? Here are a few ways to engage the press if you're on a tight budget:

- **HARO (Help a Reporter Out):** This is an e-mail that comes directly to your in-box three times a day if you subscribe. There are numerous inquiries from reporters looking for experts to interview for stories they are writing. The categories are not all specific to beauty or makeup, but there are occasions where someone is looking for makeup advice. Browsing through HARO can be laborious, but if you have time, it may be worth checking out. There may be an inquiry in your immediate area. For more details, visit the website at www.helpareporter.com.

- **Contacting local magazine editors and TV stations:** The best way to wrangle up some press is to introduce yourself to those reporters and journalists in your area who write and report about style. Your local morning show and regional magazines are always in need of content, and you might be just what they're looking for. You might even suggest a story or TV segment on beauty they hadn't thought of. Make your introduction by phone or e-mail to let them know you're interested and available to help them out with any beauty-related stories they might have in mind.

- **Sending out promotional kits:** You might also consider putting together a promotional kit to send to potential clients, magazine and newspaper editors, TV producers, and radio stations, just to let them know about you. You can include your résumé, a short biography, press clippings, photos of your work, articles you've written, or anything else relevant to your work as a makeup artist. You may not have all of these items in the beginning, but you could write about your interest in makeup, how it inspires you, and what your goals are in the beauty industry. Remember that the idea behind a promotional kit is to introduce yourself. You're selling yourself, so now is not the time to be shy. You want to let people know what makes you unique, and why they should be interested in what you have to say. Your goal is to get a callback, so if you have specific ideas, include them in your kit. If you're sending the kit to potential clients, invite them for a makeover. If you want to write an article for your local newspaper, then give them some fresh ideas on beauty topics. You get the idea.

Tracking and Targeting Your Marketing Efforts

How do you know if all the time and money you've put into marketing is working? How do you track which marketing efforts are winners and which ones are not? Well, there is an answer, and it's an online program called Google Analytics that will help you track where all of the traffic to your website or blog is coming from. It's free to install and will give you very specific information and graphs on where your business is coming from. On Google Analytics you can track:

- how many people visited your website on any given day,
- what cities and countries your visitors are from,

- which websites are sending traffic directly to your site,
- and whether the traffic on your website is trending up or down.

This is a tool I use all of the time. In fact, I check it every morning to see how many hits I had the day before and where they came from. I can easily see which websites are sending potential business my way and which ones are not. As a result of Google Analytics, I discontinued advertising on some sites and have increased my advertising on others. It's clearly a valuable tool, and best of all, there's no investment. You just need to set up your account and paste the code into your website or blog and you're up and running. If you're not very tech-savvy, then have whoever is building or managing your website add the code for you. To find out more about Google Analytics and how to install it, you can visit www.google.com/analytics.

08 Networking

If I can impress one thing upon you, it's that the business of being a makeup artist is all about networking. They always say it's not *what* you know, but *who* you know, and in this case, it's true. Makeup artistry is all about people, and referrals. That's how you'll build your business. You'll never get a job sending out a résumé or searching the want ads. Being a makeup artist means you have to get out there and make your own opportunities. They won't come to you; you have to find them. The good news is, in this age of fast-paced technology, the opportunities to network and your ability to reach people have opened up outside of your immediate area. You can now network as far and wide as you'd like, and that's exactly what you should do.

Networking the Old-Fashioned Way

There's just no replacement for it. Sure, there are other ways to network, and we'll talk about those, but old-fashioned networking has been working well for generations for a reason. People want to know who they are working with. Your personality plays as much into being a makeup artist as your talent and skill. If people like you, they are more likely to book you. It's that simple.

So, where do you start? The answer is, get out there and start meeting people, sooner rather than later. When I first opened my studio, a good friend invited twenty of her friends to celebrate at my grand opening. It was a fun girls' night out of food, drinks, and beauty. I didn't know the other women, so it was the perfect way to start networking. All of them at some point have made appointments with me, and even better than that, some of the friends of the friends have also booked appointments. They say one person will tell ten others, so keep that in mind. There's nothing more valuable than meeting people. It's without question the biggest return on your investment, which is really just your time.

There are so many ways to meet people. You don't have to throw an elaborate grand opening party, or even anything directly related to your business. Every time you step out that door there's an opportunity to meet someone new and tell them what you do. Here are a few suggestions of places to get started:

- **Friends and family:** This seems so obvious I really shouldn't have to say it, but it really is the first place to start, and it couldn't be any easier than that. Consider hosting a party and have everyone you know invite someone new. My personal experience proved that it brought a lot of business, and it was my first step in getting out there.
- **Your workplace:** If you currently have a job, whether it's full-time or part-time, let everyone there know you are now doing makeup. Offer incentives for booking an appointment with you, or simply make sure they have a brochure or business card to keep on hand. There are no rules; the idea is just to make sure you tell everyone you know.
- **Chamber of commerce:** Almost every city or town will have a chamber of commerce or some sort of business organization, and many of them will host networking events. This is a great opportunity to meet other business owners. Some of them may need makeup services themselves, or may have a clientele that would be interested.
- **Churches and schools:** If you or your children are involved in church or school activity, that is the perfect place to start spreading the word. If you have children and they participate in any of these activities, let the teachers and other mothers know about your services.
- **Play dates, book and garden clubs, or other women's groups:** Do you have a hobby or special interest that keeps you busy? Network in the groups where you spend your free time.
- **The gym:** Turn that dreaded spin class into an opportunity. Post a flyer or leave some postcards in the locker room.
- **High schools, colleges, and universities:** We all know that tweens, teens, and co-eds are as enthusiastic about beauty as we are. Offer your services for proms, sweet sixteen parties, and sorority dances.

Utilizing Social Media to Build Your Business

Social media . . . what is that? Well, if you've been living in the dark ages and aren't familiar with social media sites like Facebook and Twitter, they are online sites that allow you to connect and keep up with your friends, family, and, in some cases, people and businesses you don't even know. You can think of it as cyber networking instead of networking the old-fashioned, face-to-face way. Social networking sites allow you to expand your circle and spread the word about your business without ever leaving the house. What could be easier than that?

The two social media sites I've found most useful are Facebook and Twitter. They both work differently, so we'll take a look at both and how you can use each of them to your advantage.

Facebook

Let's start with what you may already have, which is a personal Facebook page. This is where most people are already connecting with their friends and family. You can leave updates on your page about anything that might be going on in your life; you can post photos and videos, and add links to other websites you want to share. It's really a place for you to share what's new in your life. What a perfect place to announce your new adventure as a makeup artist! You can post the link to your new website and blog, announce specials and promotions, post videos, press, and blog posts. Anything you would want to tell someone in person can be posted on Facebook for everyone to

A Facebook Snapshot

- There are more than 750 million active users.

- The average user has 130 friends.

- People spend over 700 billion minutes per month on Facebook.

- There are over 900 million objects that people interact with (pages, groups, events, and community pages).

- The average user is connected to 80 community pages, groups, and events.

- There are more than 30 billion pieces of content (web links, news stories, blog posts, notes, photo albums, etc.) shared each month.

see. The great thing about using the site is that not only will your friends and family see updates and announcements, but they can "share" this information with all of *their* Facebook friends. The more of your friends that share your updates, the more exposure you'll get. It's the same concept as "six degrees of separation."

So your personal page is great for sharing with people you already know, but how do you network with people you don't know? Well, there are Facebook pages created just for businesses where people can interact with you and hear all about your business without "requesting" to be your friend. They can simply "like" your page. It's ideal for anyone who takes an interest in your makeup artistry and doesn't know you personally.

I'd recommend having both a personal page (for your friends and family) and a business page (for those who don't know you). The more people you can interact with, the better.

Here are some ideas on how to best use your Facebook business page:

- Post photos and create albums of your work.
- Post behind-the-scenes photos of you working.
- Offer makeup tips and tricks.
- Offer promotions, specials, and discounts.
- Run giveaways or contests.
- Update your page with projects you're working on, like photo shoots.
- Link to other websites where your work may be featured, like photography blogs or online publications.
- Add a link to your blog posts (you can manually or automatically have your blog posts added to your pages).

Tips on Setting Up Facebook

Setting up a Facebook page is simple and straightforward. Go to www.facebook.com to sign up and get started.

When you're setting up both your personal and business pages, I strongly recommend creating a custom URL, sometimes referred to as a "vanity URL." This is a good idea for two reasons. First, it means that people will be able to find you more quickly, and your address will be easier for them to remember. Second, your Facebook pages will show up in search results, like Google, and having your name in the web address will be added-value to the search engines. A custom URL looks like this:

- www.facebook.com/yourname (personal)
- www.facebook.com/businessname (business page)

There are a few things to keep in mind. You will want to create your personal page with a custom URL first. Facebook requires that the administrator (meaning you, the creator) of a Facebook business page have a personal page first before creating a custom URL for a business page. They also require that you have at least twenty-five "fans" before you can create your custom URL.

Networking on Facebook

Okay, so you've set up your new Facebook pages; now, how do you use Facebook as a networking tool? Well, to fully take advantage of Facebook, you need to seek out other people and businesses that you want to connect with. Are there photographers or wedding planners you'd like to work with? Are there makeup artists you'd like to assist? You get the idea. Networking on Facebook is no different than introducing yourself for the first time at a party or networking in person. You just have to put yourself out there. There are several ways to introduce yourself and make new connections:

- "Like" other businesses; it shows that you admire or appreciate their work.
- Add other businesses to your page to show your interest and affiliation.
- "Comment" on pages or posts in your news feed. This shows you're interested in what someone is doing or saying.
- "Like" or "Share" a post. Liking or sharing a post means that everyone in your news feed will see that information.
- Send a Facebook "message" to introduce yourself directly.
- Post a greeting on their "wall."

And if all of this sounds like Greek to you, there's a quick primer on Facebook "speak" (so to speak) below.

Other Facebook Features

These are a few other features that you also might find useful.

1. **Create an event:** Similar to an Evite, you can invite your Facebook "friends" to any event you're having, like a makeup party or girls' night out.
2. **Networked blogs:** This is an application on Facebook that allows you to promote your blog and permits their large community of bloggers and blog readers to see your post.
3. **Facebook ads:** You may have noticed advertisements on your Facebook page. These are sponsored ads, similar to the Google AdWords we already

Useful Facebook Terms and Definitions

Status update: In its simplest form, the status update is a report of what you're doing right now. Your status update can be a statement or a question, and can include a link to a video, photo, or blog post.

Wall: A wall is a section in your profile where others can write messages to you. It is a public writing space so others who view your profile can see what has been written on your wall. Once you have received a wall message, you can respond directly back to the friend who left it using the "wall-to-wall" mode.

Pages: This is a public profile on Facebook used by businesses, celebrities, and public groups and brands that allows your customers to follow you and interact with you.

Like: An option on Facebook to provide feedback on the stories that appear in your friend's news feed. The "like" option allows you to acknowledge a friend's news-feed item in a positive way without needing to add actual commentary.

News feed: A news feed is a list of updates on your own Facebook home page that will show updates about those people who are in your friends list. The news feed is actually a collection of events from your friends' own mini-feed that is intended to give you a quick look at what your friends have been doing on Facebook.

discussed, and are another option for targeted advertising. You create an ad based on your target market and decide how much to pay. You can direct people to your Facebook business page, or your website. Here are some of the features and benefits of a Facebook ad:

- You have the ability to connect with over 750 million potential customers. You make the ad as targeted or as broad as you want.
- You choose who sees your ad. You create an ad based on your potential client's profile, including her location, age, and interests.
- You can test different layouts, including images and text, and use the ad that works best.
- You can promote either your Facebook page, and get more "likes," or direct people to your website.
- You can use the "like" button to increase your ad's influence.
- You set the budget so the ad is affordable for you.
- You can change or adjust the budget at any time.
- You choose how people pay: per click (CPC= Cost Per Click), or every time they see your ad (CPM=Cost Per Thousand Impressions).

Twitter

And then there's Twitter—a little newer than Facebook in the world of social media, but also a powerful networking tool. It differs from Facebook in that anyone can follow you and you can follow anyone back. You don't have to send a request or know the person at all. Do you love a particular movie star or musician? Cool. You can follow them on Twitter and get all of their updates. Do you like to stay on top of breaking news? Great. Follow your favorite news station. Do you love a particular brand of clothing? You can follow them too. Twitter is broad and vast, and the ability to reach a large number of people is there. And you can do all of this from your computer or mobile phone.

Here is how Twitter explains it: "Twitter is a service for friends, family, and coworkers to communicate and stay connected through the exchange of quick, frequent messages. People write short updates, often called 'tweets,' of 140 characters or fewer. These messages are posted to your profile or your blog, sent to your followers, and are searchable on Twitter search."

And how is this useful for you? In the same way you can connect and communicate with people you don't know through your Facebook business page, the same applies to Twitter. Your messages should be short and sweet, and should let your followers know what you're up to. Your followers will want to hear about your jobs as a makeup artist, so keep them informed.

And how exactly is this considered networking? Well, is there a photographer or wedding planner you're interested in working with? Or is there a clothing store or local boutique that you'd like to connect with? Following them on Twitter is just like an introduction. You can communicate with them through a direct message, or "tweet" with them using your phone or computer, and start building a relationship before you ever meet in person.

Connecting Facebook and Twitter

Is this all too overwhelming? It certainly is a lot to learn, but taking the time to set it up is well worth the effort. If you just can't imagine managing all of this social media in addition to your real life, there is a way to get the most out of both Facebook and Twitter. You can actually connect the two. Do you prefer to Facebook? Then you can connect Twitter to receive the same updates on your Facebook business page. Or are you attached at the hip to your phone and love to tweet? Then connect your Facebook page updates to your tweets. You decide. Just keep in mind that Twitter only allows 140 characters or less, so keep your updates short.

Just remember that if you're using these social media sites to promote yourself, you'll want to keep your tweets professional and relevant to your business as a makeup artist. These sites are public domain, so everything you put out there will be there for a long time.

Promote Your Social Media Sites

- Add Facebook and Twitter icons to your website and blog so potential clients can interact with you.

- Create a customized signature for the bottom of your e-mails, and include a link to your Facebook business page and Twitter account.

- Include your Facebook and Twitter addresses on your marketing materials (postcards, brochures, and business cards).

Creating Partnerships and Getting Referrals

Networking with other businesses can really be the key to long-term success. More than just networking, it's creating mutually beneficial relationships and working partnerships. The old theory of "You scratch my back, I'll scratch yours" may have been around for a while, but it sure is a good one. The bottom line is, it's much easier to market yourself to another business than it is to individuals. Reaching each and every one of your potential clients on your own would require either a ridiculously lush advertising budget, or an enormous amount of time spent pounding the pavement. Either way, it's a huge investment of both time and money, and if you're like me, you may not have a huge reservoir of either one. Engaging with already-established businesses that cater to your type of clientele can increase your exposure better than any advertising campaign ever could. Their referrals are priceless.

Forging ahead and creating relationships is really crucial. You'll spend less on advertising, which means more money in your pocket, and you'll have longevity. What could be better than that? In one of my first attempts to reach out to the wedding industry, I was invited to a party thrown by a popular wedding planner. I met photographers, florists, stationers, caterers, boutique owners, and everyone else under the sun. Just by attending that one party, I started getting referrals and forging new friendships and partnerships with the vendors I met. I've since reduced my advertising budget to almost zero, and my bridal business continues to grow. Get out there. Make friends and create relationships.

Creative Networking

Creative industries, like makeup artistry, often require creative thinking outside of the obvious task of face painting. This includes ways to meet people. We touched briefly on several ways to market yourself in chapter 7 that fall outside the realm of traditional marketing, and one of the other benefits of some of these promotional ideas is networking. Meeting, getting to know, and collaborating with other creatives is an essential part of the business.

Photo Shoots

Let's look first at photo shoots. We already know why doing them is good for your portfolio, but an equally important benefit is meeting people. You should really think of it as targeted marketing. Not only are you marketing your work and your services, but you're also marketing yourself, and we already know that your personality is one of the keys to success. Even if the photo shoot is unpaid, which many of them are, give it your best and your efforts will come back to you as referrals from the photographer. They may have a corporate job coming up where they'll need a makeup artist, or headshots for an aspiring actor or model, or even a bride. The point is, any chance you have to do makeup, the answer should always be "yes." In fact, I spent a whole year saying yes. My goal that year was to accept every offer that came my way, paid or unpaid, with some people I knew and many that I did not. And it paid off in spades. I ended up going on two paid trips to Costa Rica in exchange for my services, met many photographers who referred countless clients and brides, and came away with material for my website, portfolio, and blog, which in the end turned into money. It seems a little odd to give your services away for free, but when you realize that it will come back to you in contacts and referrals, it makes it all worthwhile. And you're a makeup artist, after all; at the very least, photo shoots should be fun!

Guest-Blogging

If you enjoy blogging, another way to network online is referred to as "guest-blogging." It really means that you're writing posts that will be seen on another person's blog. For example, a respected wedding planner was creating a fashion and style section for her blog and asked me to write posts for her on bridal beauty. Guest-blogging has many benefits: The first is building a valued relationship with the person you're guest-blogging for. They obviously respect your work if they've asked you to write posts for them, so nurturing that relationship is important. Your efforts will come back to you in referrals, and you will also create some articles for those promotional kits we talked about. The other upside is that her client base will get to know you, and again, hopefully, some of those readers will turn into clients. And don't forget: If you have a blog, consider inviting someone you admire to guest-blog for you—perhaps a hair stylist, skin-care specialist, or local fashion expert. You'll be attracting a new client base to your blog and building a relationship with someone new.

TV Appearances

I'm sure many of you watch your local morning or afternoon news, and many of your stations feature lifestyle or style segments from time to time. Approaching your local station to do beauty segments is another way to build relationships and do some networking. What a powerful tool television can be when it comes to creating awareness of your business! A single segment can reach a large audience, and meeting and working with producers and crew at the station is a valuable way to build relationships within the media. One segment could lead to your becoming a regular contributor (which is what happened to me).

Don't Forget! Clients Are Everywhere

I've offered some ways to network in this section, both traditional and nontraditional. Some of these methods may appeal to you more than others, but by sharing what has worked for me, I hope that you'll take away a few key ideas: Meeting people and networking is the one and only way that you will get jobs. There are opportunities and clients right around the corner, waiting for you. All you have to do is be open and realize that every chance you have to meet someone new is another chance to do what you love.

What is it like to be a client, the one having her makeup done? Have you ever had your makeup done by someone else? What was it like for you? Did you enjoy it, or was it stressful? Were you happy with the end result? I think we've all been there, in the makeup chair, at the mercy and the whims of the makeup artist. Maybe the finished look was good, maybe it wasn't. Perhaps it was what you had in mind, but quite possibly, it was not. Makeup artistry is, after all, art. And art is subjective. Everyone's idea of beauty is different. So how do you create the perfect look for each client and make sure they leave happy? A lot of that has to do with the steps you take before you ever lift a brush.

Your Personal Presentation

We've spent a lot of time talking about the actual craft of makeup artistry, the particulars of setting up your business, and the client and her likes and dislikes, but let's keep in mind that *you* are the client's first impression of your brand. Your personal appearance will give her a first impression of you, and she'll make judgments about you before she ever sits in your chair. I know it sounds harsh but it's just the cold, hard truth. Your personal appearance and the way you present yourself can quite possibly make or break the client experience for someone. Now, am I saying you need to look like a supermodel or wear pricey designer clothes to be a makeup artist? Absolutely not. I don't want you to look or be anything more than your best self. In fact, I think the most successful artists are themselves 100 percent of the time. Remember, your personality is one-third of the puzzle, and the more your personal presentation reflects your personality, the better.

The most important things to remember are very basic—things you may not have thought of unless you've ever been on the receiving end of a makeup appointment gone wrong. Here are a few things to consider to make sure your client enjoys her time with you. Remember, you are working one on one with someone, in an intimate setting, and putting your best foot forward will ensure the appointment gets off to a good start.

Wardrobe

Now, I know you're a fashionista or fashionisto. I don't even have to know you to know this as truth. You probably wouldn't even be interested in this business if you didn't already care about your appearance, so I'm not going to preach on the specifics of what you should wear. I'm not your mother, and you're not five. I have complete confidence that you can put together an outfit that is professional and still reflects your personality. What I would like to point out is that you need to dress and present yourself in a way that makes sense to your client. Do you need to dress like your client? No, but if your clientele is conservative, you need to be aware of that and keep it in mind when you're meeting with them. Is your clientele young and hip? Then, there you go; you can err on the hip and trendy side. These aren't hard-and-fast rules, but the point I'm trying to make is, your appearance needs to be polished, appropriate, and approachable. If you keep these three buzzwords in mind when you're getting dressed, you'll be halfway home to a great consultation.

Jewelry

Accessories are a good way to personalize your look. I get it. I'm a girl. But there is nothing more annoying than the jingle-jangle of too many baubles and beads, especially around your wrists. Keep the bangles and clunky watches to a minimum. No, scratch that; just don't wear them at all. If your jewelry or accessories make any noise at all when you move, just don't wear them.

Cleavage

I know. This is sort of an awkward conversation, but something you might not think of until your client is staring directly down your shirt. Umm, slightly uncomfortable. So, in order to prevent any awkward moments between you and your new client, be aware of how much your girls are showing. Unfortunately that barstool or director's chair you just purchased is directly at eye level with hopefully one of your best assets. And boys, this applies to you too. Keep in mind that your client may be staring directly at your chest. No matter how toned you are, tight shirts and peekaboo chest hair may be off-putting to your client. In other words, keep your dress professional, folks.

Nails

Oh the manicure/pedicure . . . it's my favorite sport. Okay, let's be honest. It's my only sport. And many of you may be right there with me. But here's the thing: Your nails have to be short. No discussion. And I don't just mean kind of short. In an ideal world, your nails wouldn't come above your fingertips; that means no white will show above the tip of your finger. No fake nails with fancy designs, no French manicures, no rounded, pointed talons. Plain Jane, short, polished nails are the only appropriate nails to have. Why? The last thing you want to do is scratch your client with your freshly painted claws. End of story.

Fragrance

We've all been there, in the grocery store or the back of a taxi, when a waft of unfortunately cloying fragrance blows your way. It's offensive, strong, and lingers well past the end of the party. It's not to say you can't wear a bit of your signature scent; just keep it light, and remember that the distance between you and your client at some points during the makeup process will be mere inches.

Smoking

Okay, it's not my thing, and I won't judge you if it's yours. But keep in mind, those of us who don't smoke can be extra sensitive and can pick up the scent like a specially trained retriever. If you are a smoker, just be aware that smoke can be an offensive problem for a client. Make sure your garments are laundered and smoke-free, and do your best to refrain from smoking right before and during your makeup session. You'll essentially be breathing all over your client for an hour, so keep it fresh.

Mints

Smokers and nonsmokers alike, beware—coffee, garlicky food, and other breath-busters should be avoided before and during your consultation. Keep a tin of mints nearby and have as many of them as it takes to make you feel confident. Your client may benefit from a few, too, so always do the polite thing and offer them around.

Personal Space

This is tricky. There's no question that you'll be up close and personal with every client, but being aware of just *how* close and personal is important. I can't tell you how many times a new artist has straddled my knee as they tried to find the right angle to apply whatever they were trying to apply. Please, please, please, remember your client is there for a makeover, not a lap dance.

Be Mannerly

Now, I'm from the South. As a people, we're known for being very mannerly, so this is my chance to preach just a little bit more. Sorry; if there wasn't a reason to preach, I wouldn't be bothered.

Talking and Texting

I know how much you love your phone. It's your connection to the outside world. In some cases, it may be the only way you communicate with the world, but for a client, it's distracting and just plain rude if you're engaging with your phone in any way. If you just can't stay away, put it in your purse, leave it in the car, or just don't bring it with you at all. No talking, no texting, no ringing, at all. Ever. You wouldn't want someone on the phone if you were expecting their undivided attention, so extend the same courtesy to your clients. If you have to have your phone nearby, make sure the ringer is off.

Language

Depending on the crowd seeking out your services for makeup, you might encounter some occasional harsh language, not fit for publication. Now, I'm no dirty-word virgin, and that kind of language rarely offends me, but as a professional makeup artist, the mannerly thing to do is not engage is trashy talk back. While your client is free to be herself, it's your job to keep your end of the conversation rated G—PG at the most. Hopefully everyone who books you will be respectful, but in the event a potty mouth sneaks its way in your door, keep it light and clean.

Don't Overshare

If you haven't figured it out yet, a makeup artist is part beauty magician, therapist, confidante, and life coach. For some reason, sitting in the makeup chair makes ordinarily closed-up women want to share their personal troubles and triumphs. Rumor has it they do the same thing in the hair-salon chair, but that's another discussion. In any case, you may find that you learn more about your client than you had ever expected, and, like a good therapist, the best thing you can do is listen. Even though she may want to share with you, that doesn't mean you need to share all of your intimate details with her. Keep your personal troubles and tribulations to yourself. Don't overshare your personal life, and keep your interactions with your client positive, light, and upbeat.

Now that you're feeling pretty, polished, and 100 percent yourself, let's move forward and take a look at the next steps of the client experience.

Responding to Inquiries

You've spent a great deal of time marketing and promoting yourself, networking every chance you get, and Facebooking and blogging until your eyes cross. Finally, you have inquiries. Whether it's for a makeup lesson or for a bridal trial, it's important to make sure to respond to that inquiry in a polite, professional manner. If you're working from home and using either your cell phone or home landline, make sure that your voice-mail message greeting is professional and states your business name, hours of operation, and the best way to reach you or leave a message if you're not available. Clients may be uncomfortable leaving a message on what sounds like a personal line. And chances are, if you're just starting this adventure and aren't yet committed to it full-time, you won't have the luxury of sitting by the phone, waiting for a call. Be clear and concise when you return calls, whether in person or in the form of a voice-mail message.

My preference for responding to inquiries is by e-mail, so my voice-mail message asks the caller to please e-mail me the details of their inquiry. Of course I return phone calls too, but if you have a preference and it's easier for you to be reached one way over another, it's important to state that, especially since there are so many ways for people to get in touch. If you know you can only respond to inquiries in the evening, then state that in your message. Be as clear and concise as you can so potential clients know what to expect.

Booking Appointments

All right! You've finally made contact with someone who is interested in your services. Just be aware that some may be calling for general information, or simply shopping around to find someone. If you're lucky, some callers may actually be ready to book an appointment with you. You'll need to ask some questions first, to find out exactly what they are looking for before you jump into appointment scheduling.

Here are a few questions you may want to ask in your initial conversations with them, if they haven't already offered the information on their own. I'm not trying to direct your phone calls—just letting you know some of the questions that come up for me on a regular basis.

- How did you hear about me? Did you find me through a referral, online, or through my advertising?
- What type of service are you looking for? Bridal, makeup lesson, makeup application, etc.
- Have you ever had your makeup done professionally before?
- What did you like, or not like, about that experience?
- Is there a particular look you are trying to achieve?
- How many in your bridal party will be needing makeup?

After gathering all of the information you need, make sure to give them a quote for the service they're interested in, especially if your rates aren't posted on your website or marketing materials. Make sure your quote includes travel fees or extras, like lashes.

Meeting the Client: Asking the Right Questions

Great! She's booked an appointment. You may have some preliminary information about her and why she's interested in your services, but the more you know about her past experiences and what her expectations are for her appointment with you, the easier it will be for you to make sure she leaves with a good experience. This is where you'll need to start doing some detective work—a little beauty sleuthing, if you will. You need to ask a lot of questions. Whether you're applying her makeup for a special event, giving her a lesson, cleaning out her makeup products, or creating her bridal look, you need to know what she has in mind. You need to know:

- **Has she had her makeup done before?** What did she like about the look, and what didn't she like? She may have had several experiences with other makeup artists, so the more information you can get about what worked for her and what didn't, the better. You don't want to repeat someone else's mistakes.
- **What are her favorite makeup products?** What formulas does she like and not like? Some clients may be attached to certain products. Some of them you may agree with and some of them you may not. Finding out her preferences will make the application run smoother. For example, some women like full-coverage foundation while others prefer a sheer finish. Get all of those little details.
- **What colors is she comfortable wearing?** Some women are only comfortable wearing neutrals and some are open to wearing more color. You'll need to determine where she fits in and if she's open to new color suggestions and combinations outside of her comfort zone. If she has her makeup with her, ask to see the products and colors she's already using.
- **How is she using the products and colors she already owns?** I like to have every client talk me through her process so I know what techniques she's been using—the right ones and the wrong ones. This helps me know where I can make improvements and where I need to explain why something works and why something doesn't.
- **What is her lifestyle like?** You don't want to create a super-glammed-up look for a mom of three who just needs a natural day look. Find out what her lifestyle is like and how much time she's willing to commit to her makeup each day.
- **What type of look is she trying to achieve?** It may be a natural everyday look, a polished business look, or something more glamorous for evening. Make sure you have an idea what she has in mind. You can ask her to bring photos from magazines of looks she likes and start from there, or you can create your own "look book" to have on hand. Compile looks that you like

from magazines and let your clients flip through the book for inspiration. Include looks that range from natural to glam and will appeal to a wide variety of clients.

I know this sounds like a lot of interrogating and information gathering, but trust me, the more information and direction you have, the better the end result will be. You want her to be happy, and short of mind reading, you need to know what she's thinking.

Listen, Listen, Listen

All the asking in the world won't do you any good if you're not listening. And when I say *listening,* I mean you really need to "hear" what your client is saying. Some clients may have a specific look in mind and may have a hard time articulating what that look is. One woman's natural eye is another woman's smoky eye. It's your job to interpret what she's saying and translate it into a makeup look that makes sense for her. You should feel comfortable and confident enough that if you're unclear as to what she's looking for, repeat it back for some clarification, or tell her what you "heard" and ask her if that's what she meant. I know it sounds remedial, but this is one of the biggest challenges of being a makeup artist: interpreting what your client is saying and then translating it into a look that makes her happy. Remember, you can't see what she's visualizing in her mind, and she can't see the direction you have in mind for her, so *listen, listen, listen* before you start a makeup application.

Offering Your Professional Opinion

You may have "heard" everything she just said, and you may be crystal clear about the look she's going for, but you still don't think it's the right look for her. What on earth do you do? You know what? It's okay. Offering your opinion as a professional makeup artist is part of the consultation process. If you've asked all the right questions and determined a direction that might be right for her, it's perfectly reasonable and, most of the time, expected, for you to make suggestions. If she's come to you with a level of confidence and trust, your suggestions should be welcome. In the end, she still might want to try the look she had in mind, and that's okay, too. There's always an experimental aspect to makeup—it's painting, after all—and thankfully, it washes right off. Trying a look and changing your mind later is sometimes part of the game.

The most important part of offering your opinion is having a good reason behind it, along with the ability to explain how and why you think something works for her. People only seek out experts when they feel like what they've been doing on their own isn't working. I often offer to try more than one look on a client. I'll do half the face in the look she had in mind and the other half in the way I had in mind. The majority of the time, I've been able to show her something new that she likes. If someone still insists on a look you don't agree with, as long as she is happy with the results, then that's what counts. As an example, I had a client come to me for a makeup lesson. We looked through all of the products she had and discussed which ones were working and which ones were not. By the end of the appointment, we'd created a look for her that she was happy with. The only caveat is, I couldn't talk her out of layering three, yes, three, foundations to get the coverage she wanted. No one needs that much coverage, and there's absolutely no good reason to be using more than one foundation. But what could I do? It was her choice to take my advice or not. The point is, you need to listen to your client's needs, offer your professional opinion, but always keep in mind, it's her face, not yours, and your ultimate goal is to make her happy.

Tips for a Smooth Makeup Application

Okay, you're finally ready to get to work doing the fun stuff! It's just what you've been waiting for. There are a few things you can do during the makeup application process to ensure that your client has a good experience and loves her new look.

One of the first things you should do is to pull out a collection or range of colors that you think will work for her, based on the conversation you just had. Showing her the colors before you get started will confirm that you're on the right track and that you understand the look she wants. This will also give her some visual reference when she's purchasing colors on her own.

The next thing to be aware of is your touch. It may sound strange, but I don't think many artists realize that how you approach and touch the client is an important part of the experience. Be light with your touch. No one likes to feel they're being poked with a makeup brush, and trust me, I've had those experiences. It's uncomfortable, and it doesn't build any confidence or trust in the artist. In fact, it does just the opposite. The person in the makeup chair starts to feel that the artist doesn't have full control of their brushes. One of the best things you can do when you're practicing on friends and family is to get feedback from them. Ask specifically if they're comfortable with your touch during the application.

No one wants to feel like they're being pawed at, either. You will definitely need to touch the client during the session, but do your best to use your brushes and not lean your hand all over the client's face. I learned a trick many moons ago that has served me well, and goes a long way toward making the client feel comfortable while you're applying her makeup. Keep a powder puff handy, and if you have to touch their face to get a good angle, use the puff as a "pillow" between your hand and their face. I secure the puff on my pinkie finger. It also comes in handy if you have to do a little cleanup here and there.

You'll also have to become somewhat of a conductor during the makeup application. You'll need the client to look up, look down, to the right, to the left, and every direction in between. Be clear about what you need them to do in order to get the best application. You may even need to turn their head or lift their chin. I often joke that I have more hand signals than the most experienced flight attendants, but, hey, it works.

Now here's a biggie: applying mascara. You can certainly understand why some people would be slightly squeamish with a pointy wand so close to their eyes. I've noticed that new artists often struggle with this step. Have the client look directly over your shoulder, and then halfway down. You may find your own technique, but this has worked comfortably for me. I can get the wand right into the lashes from underneath and from above. Wiggle the brush into the base of the lashes and then brush the mascara out the length of the lashes, first from below, and next from the top. Presto! Mascara is on, even on clients who are "blinkers."

So you've completed the makeup application and it's time to show her the new look—the big reveal. Now, you may or may not have given her a mirror to watch the process as you went along, but either way, I would encourage you to have the client see her new look in different mirrors and in different lighting situations. Natural light is always the best, and if you have the chance to apply someone's makeup near a window, that's always preferable to artificial lighting, even when it's the large-scale makeup lights. Either way, I always take the client outside with a hand mirror so they can see how they will look in natural light. That's always the best test of a makeup application. If their makeup looks good outside, it will look good anywhere.

Handling Objections

And now it's time for her feedback. You've listened to her needs and worked hard to create the perfect look. You love it, but will she? In a beauty utopia, everyone would waltz away from your makeup chair singing your praises, elated that she looks twenty years younger. But sadly, that's not always the case. Every once in a while you may not get the positive reaction you're hoping for, and if that happens, don't fret. Many women have a hard time seeing themselves another way. She may be that woman who's been stuck in a beauty rut since the Nixon era and is having a hard time parting with her old beauty identity, or she may be just a little insecure about shedding her old skin and wearing a new one, so to speak.

Every artist experiences this, and how they handle negative feedback is what sets the novices apart from the professionals. Ask how she feels about the look and get some feedback from her. If she seems hesitant, let her know you're not going to be offended; you want to make sure she's happy. Let her know that anything she's not sure about can be changed. Listen to her concerns, and if you're not clear, repeat them back to her for clarification. And then cheerfully make the corrections. Simple. Usually a little tweak here and a little tweak there is all it takes to make sure the look is perfect.

And what if she's still not sure? Encourage her to wear the look for the day. In many cases, it just takes a little time for someone to start seeing themselves in a new light. Or you can suggest she show her new look to a friend. There's nothing more convincing than an objective opinion from a close friend. Either way, whether you're able to handle her objections and make the right changes, or she leaves still unsure about her new appearance, if you've done your very best to make her look and feel good, then you've done your job.

Interpreting and Translating Trends

Trends. This is a word we hear every season, every time the winds change. In makeup, a concept that may be fun doesn't always work on everyone. Trends come and go, but your face is here to stay, and you always want to look your best. Wearing every makeup trend that comes along just might make you look like the neighborhood girl on the prowl, if you know what I mean. In any case, translating and interpreting trends is an important skill to develop. As many times as I've preached that your face isn't the best place to demonstrate your trendy side, every season, clients are looking for ways to change and freshen up their look. New clothes, freshly colored and coiffed hair, and new makeup. It's a no-brainer. So how do you go about coming up with fresh ideas, managing to both follow the trends and make them wearable for the average woman? This is where your creativity comes into play.

all have piles of fashion and beauty magazines, and if you've been developing
ft, you probably read them like an Iron Chef reads cookbooks. To be honest,
ven actually read them, I just look at the makeup. I check out the editorial
, the ad campaigns, and the celebrity features. Like me, I'm sure you often see
looks that you love while recognizing that they don't often work in the real world.
Bold colors, vampy lips, extreme techniques—all appropriately fun for your next
photo shoot, but what about your clients? How can you take these extreme fashion
looks and adapt them to have a little fun from season to season?

Here are some recurring trends that everyone wants to try and some suggestions
for translating them into wearable, everyday looks.

Bold, Vibrant Lipstick

One of the newest trends within the last few seasons is a bright red or boldly colored
matte or creme lipstick. Many women are already used to wearing some color on
their lips, but generally not in shades of bright red, coral, and fuchsia, and certainly
not in matte or full-coverage formulas. Generally clients are more comfortable wearing softer, more neutral shades.

If your client has beautiful lips with the perfect cupid's bow, has a bold, quirky
personality, or loves vintage looks, introducing her to the bright lipstick shades of the
season may be just what she needs to update her look. With bold lips, just make sure
to keep the eyes soft. Try icy pastels or shimmery neutrals on the eyes.

For a client who is more mature, has small lips, or is just uncomfortable wearing
bold lip color, introduce her to sheer formulas of the trendy, bold colors. Brighter
shades of lip gloss and sheer lipsticks and tints can be an easy way to introduce color
without too much shock. The sheerer the formula, the less intense the color will be,
and the more likely it is your client will embrace and wear the trend.

Colorful, Bright Eyes

On the flip side of the coin, trendy bright eye colors show up on the runway and the
magazines every season. A dramatic eye seems like it would be fun to wear, but the
moment you hit the street, you're all of a sudden back in that streetwalker category.
Fashion colors are enticing when you're shopping, too. It's fun to load up your professional makeup kit with all the glittery, colorful pots of paint that are out there on the
market, but in reality, you rarely get to use them because they're just not appropriate
for average folks.

So, creating a fashion-forward eye for your client can sometimes be a challenge, especially if her preference is for that boring palette of neutrals. To introduce and incorporate bright color on the eyes, try using a liner in a fashion color and keeping very tight to the lash line, almost like a little peekaboo of color. Keep the rest of the eye neutral and within her comfort zone. Or try using an eye shadow in a bright color and again, smudge it right along the lash line. Combining brights with neutrals is the best way to get your client to experiment with color. In this case, a little goes a long way. Also try to keep in mind shades that complement her eye color. Don't forget your color theory basics.

Vampy, Dark Lips

If you were around for the vampy lip trend of the nineties, then you'll know what I'm talking about: deep, dark lips, sometimes in shades of deep plum or dark, rich brown. It's a trend that has lived on and is hard for most people to pull off without looking like Elvira. Because the shades are so much darker than most people's natural lip color, it looks harsh on anyone without a dark complexion to match.

Deep lips make their way onto every runway, particularly for the fall/winter season, and they can be wearable if they're done right, and on the right person. Certainly the darker the skin tone of your client, the deeper the shade can be on their lips, but for someone with a lighter complexion who is interested in deeper colors for fall, look for sheer versions of gloss or lip tints. Also look for shades that don't have undertones that are too blue; deep burgundies, rich reds, and plums with a rosy undertone are easier to wear, and the most universal. Shades with too much blue can make the skin look sallow, and let's be honest—only dead people have blue lips. Not very flattering. If your client wants to experiment with browns, suggest neutrals that complement her natural coloring and natural lip color.

Smoky Eye

I don't know a woman alive who hasn't at some point tried or aspired to the ultimate smoky eye. (Okay, maybe a few, but in my world, they're freaks of nature.) I receive countless requests to create the perfect smoky eye for a client. It's a hot look every season, and a staple in any makeup artist's arsenal. If you can master and manipulate the infamous smoky eye, you're on your way to success.

The problem is, not everyone can create a smoky eye without having the client look like a raccoon, and most clients just don't have enough technique to apply it correctly themselves. You'll also notice as you start working consistently as a makeup artist that the smoky eye—and what it actually looks like—is different for every woman.

Using the standard black or charcoal to create a smoky eye can often be the problem; it looks too harsh for the average woman. It may look great on camera and on film, but it doesn't really translate to a wearable, everyday look. The great news is that you can create a smoky eye with any color at all. Navy, hunter green, plum, and a reddish brown can all be beautifully sexy and much softer and more wearable. Again, choose a color that complements your client's eye color.

If your client is on the conservative side, more mature, or has extremely dark circles, but still wants to try the smoky eye, create all of the definition along the top lashes only and leave the lower lash line clean. It draws the focus to the upper lashes and the iris of the eye and deemphasizes the under-eye area. You get a modified smoky look that is still beautiful and wearable.

Heavy, Dark Eyeliner

While heavy, dark eyeliner certainly makes eyes stand out in magazines, on red carpets, and on television, in the real day-to-day grind of life, it can just make us commoners look tired, washed out, and harsh. The problem is, for some reason, women continue to over-line their eyes way past the technique's expiration date. It seems to be one of the first makeup ruts many women get stuck in. Just like the smoky eye, heavy liner is aspirational; while it certainly suits those in the fashion world, it has to be modified in order to be wearable for the rest of us.

Just like the smoky eye in black, heavy eyeliner in black is hard to wear. Encourage your clients, without sounding like a broken record, to try liner in a shade that best suits their eye color. If your client prefers gel or liquid liner, suggest lining only the top lashes, leaving the bottom lash line clean. You can go stronger and thicker on the top lashes that way. If your client prefers lining both the top and the bottom, line the top lashes with gel or liquid and use an eye shadow to define the bottom lash line instead. It's softer, more flattering, and works on almost everyone. You'll also have more control over the depth of the color, depending on the shade and brush you use.

Winged Eye Shadow

Oh, that "winged" eye shadow. I know you've seen it walking the streets. It may have even turned your head, and possibly not in a good way. Again, fashion-y, yes; right for everyone, absolutely not. Extending eye shadow at the outer corner or creating "wings" at the end is fine, in moderation. It's great to apply a little upturn of color, particularly if that suits the natural shape of your client's eyes, but moving color past the crease and even up to the brow is a regular woman's beauty "don't." Again, taking an extreme look that works in the fashion world and showing your client how to adapt it to the real world is a skill. In this case, less is more.

Shimmer and Highlighting

Shimmer, sparkle, and shine always seems to make their way into the seasonal trend pool, and just like everything else, a little highlight and shine in moderation can be a beautiful thing. The problem is the overuse and abuse of shimmer. Every product that touches the client doesn't need to highlight their features like a 1970s disco ball.

Shimmer needs to be strategically placed, and where it goes will depend on your client. Her age and her preferences should all dictate where it should go (if anywhere). In general, I think the tendency is for most people to shimmer up the eyes, and that's fine, but my advice is, if you're using heavy shimmer on the lids, then skip it on the brow bone. If you're highlighting the brow bone, then keep the shimmer on the lid to a minimum. Think about it this way: If everything has shimmer on it, then nothing is really being highlighted. Choose carefully, and for more mature clients, remember that less is more; in fact, they may want to skip it altogether.

Dewy Skin

Now this is a trend that I think everyone should be on board with. I remember the days of flat, matte, heavily powdered skin, and let's be real: It just made everyone look twenty years older than they really were. Those outdated formulas of thick, liquid foundation and loose powders sit on top of the skin, settle into lines, and just look outdated. If you can see the foundation or powder on the skin, then it's time to make a change. Skin should look like skin, and fresher, dewier formulas of foundation and tinted moisturizers provide enough coverage and will give your client a healthy glow. Beautiful, healthy-looking skin should always be your goal.

The only downside is, dewy can sometimes turn to oily, and without warning. Instructing your client to use a primer before her foundation should give her the protection she needs from oil, and the slip she needs to keep the foundation from sitting on top of her skin. I've preached the benefits of primer before, and this is exactly why. Unless your client is extremely oily, you may want to skip powder altogether. Not everyone needs it, and in fact, most people don't.

10 Contracts, Payments, and Policies

Unfortunately, the business of being a makeup artist isn't all beauty and glamour. Trust me, I wish it was, but being in business for yourself also means you have to tend to the mundane and unglamorous aspects of your business. The bottom line is, we all have to get paid, or this would just be a hobby. To ensure that your business thrives, you have to establish policies, determine a client's options for payment, and in some cases, secure your time with a contract and a deposit. The first thing you'll need to do is determine how you'll operate your day-to-day transactions with clients. Let's start by looking at how you'll put your working policies into place.

Establishing Policies

Why do you need to outline your working policies? The answer is, you don't have to have any if you don't want to. Flying by the seat of your pants and being flexible in the way you work may serve you just fine in the beginning, but as your business grows, being clear in your mind and with the client about how you like to work just makes good business sense. No one will bat an eye if you have structure to your business, even if you are just a business of one. And what types of basic policies are we talking about?

- **Do you have hours of operation?** Even if you don't have a storefront, you still may have only certain hours that you're available to schedule appointments. Be clear on your voice mail and website if you have preferred hours. As an example, my website states that I am only available by appointment, and my voice mail states that phone inquiries are answered from Tuesday through Saturday from 11:00 a.m. to 4:00 p.m. While I have some flexibility, it's nice for the client to have a general idea of how and when I'll be available to them.

- **Do you have a cancellation policy?** Your client booked an appointment with you three weeks ago and then canceled the morning of the appointment. You could have filled that spot with another client, which means you've lost revenue. So, just like the doctor's office and your hair salon, you may want to create a cancellation policy. Enforcing one takes some time and effort, but if booking appointments with clients cuts into other streams of income, or you don't have much flexibility in your schedule, you may want to consider putting one in place.
- **What forms of payment do you accept?** We'll discuss your many options in this chapter. What's important is that you're clear about your preferences well before you meet with the client so they'll know what to expect and can be prepared.

In some cases, as is customary in the bridal business, you may also need to put your working policies in writing, as in a written contract. Let's take a look at where and when you would need something more formal.

Writing a Contract

Now that you've established some basic working policies, let's dig deeper and look at why, in some cases, you'll need a written contract. If you're like me, legalese and lawyer talk is about as interesting as a trip to the dentist's office. (I hate the dentist's office.) And to be completely honest, most of it doesn't even make sense to me. Unfortunately, there are times as a makeup artist when you'll need a contract to secure your time, especially if you're planning on working with brides. I'm sure you're thinking, "Why do I need a contract if I'm working with brides?"

The best way to answer this is to give you an example from my early "no contract" days. I had just opened my shop, and the first bride to call and inquire about my services had booked an appointment to come in for a trial. This was great—my first opportunity to start the bridal part of my business! The trial seemed to run smoothly, and at the end of the appointment, the bride indicated she wanted to book me for her wedding day. Although I knew from researching other makeup artists' websites that some required a signed contract and deposit to secure the date, I had never taken the time to think through why that might be.

The bride and I discussed some of the details, including timing, and she said she would be in touch with the address of where she wanted me to meet her on the day of the wedding. Days passed, and finally, the day before the wedding I realized I had no directions to her location. I called the bride to ask her where she wanted me to meet her and she sounded surprised. She said she wouldn't be needing me after all. Now that was a real head-scratcher, and an unfortunate one at that. I had booked my time for her, turning down other clients and opportunities to work. Thankfully I learned a very important lesson on this very first encounter with a bride: Get a signed contract and deposit to hold the date. If you don't, you run the risk of losing money by turning other potential clients away in the meantime.

To be honest, the situation had me a little ruffled, and I thought about it and thought about it, and thought about it again. What did I miss? The conclusion is, I didn't miss anything. Some people are true to their word and some are not. If I say I'm going to be there, then I'm going to be there, but I've learned that it doesn't always work that way for other people. Perhaps she found another makeup artist she liked better, or maybe she decided my services weren't in her budget. In hindsight, I should have asked her for answers at the time, but I was caught completely off guard and didn't press the issue. Now, I'll never know. What I do know is that my time is valuable, and I don't want to give it to someone unless they are committed. The bottom line is, unless it's someone you have a personal relationship with, you'll want to have everything in writing to protect both you and the client.

For a makeup artist, having a contract is a plus, especially when your clients (especially brides) may be booking you a year or so in advance. When you've established yourself as a reputable makeup artist and your business starts to soar, trust me, that will be the case. Having everything in writing will ensure that you know where you need to be a year from now, and what dates you have available as you get new inquiries. On the flip side, having a contract also protects your client. Remember, she doesn't know you any better than you know her. She's trusting you to be a part of the biggest day of her life, and if you don't show up, that would just be the makings of another wedding-day horror story.

So how on earth do you go about constructing a contract? Well, first you have to confirm all the specific details for the day and determine what you need in terms of deposit and policy to secure the date. This varies from artist to artist, so make sure you know what will make you comfortable first before putting it all on paper. Decide whether you're going to require just a signed contract, or a contract and a deposit. In my opinion it's wise to require a deposit of some kind. People are more likely to be fully committed if they've already given you some of their hard-earned cash. You may decide to ask for a flat rate from everyone, regardless of the total dollar amount of the services rendered, or you may decide a percentage down is better for you. Whatever you decide, here are the items I would suggest including in your contract.

- Your company name and contact information
- The name of the bride
- The date of the wedding
- The location of the wedding
- The address where you'll be doing the makeup
- The number of people in the bridal party confirmed for makeup
- The total dollar amount based on the number of people
- The deposit amount
- The balance due
- How the bride will be paying (cash, check, or charge)
- What payment types you accept
- Your return address or e-mail address. A specific date or time the contract needs to be filled out and returned to you
- Any extra services outlined, like lashes, additional hours for touch-ups, or travel fees

Take a look at the sample contract I created based on my policies, found on page 139. You'll notice several things I include that may or may not be applicable to you. First, I include a separate fee for anyone who may want to have their makeup done who was not included in the original contract. Because you're being booked so far in advance, all of the members of the bridal party may not have been confirmed for makeup. In my experience, there is always someone who wants to have their makeup done at the last minute, so I include that in the contract. You'll also notice that I give two options for a deposit. I offer a credit card hold, much like you would do to book a hotel room. I only charge the card if they cancel their services, and it gives them the option to pay the balance in full on the day of the wedding. (This obviously only works if you've decided to accept credit cards.)

The last item I want to specifically point out is at the very bottom of the contract. It is a deadline for returning the contract, and something I added only recently. Over the years, I've had more than a few brides interested in booking my services; they request a contract and then never return it. Again, this just left me wondering whether I should hold the date or release it and book someone else. So again, just for clarity and the need to keep my schedule in check, I allow a small window for them to return the contract before I offer the date to someone else.

My contract is in no way a master copy or a format that will work for everyone; it's just an example of how you can create and customize one for yourself. What if you're not comfortable putting one together for yourself? There are several other options for you to consider. If you have a budget, then certainly you can consult a practicing lawyer in your area. You can also contact one of your local colleges, universities, or law schools. Many of them have programs that will aid small businesses or individuals with simple legal matters like writing contracts. And lastly, there are inexpensive services available online, like www.legalzoom.com, that offer standardized contracts or access to a licensed lawyer who can create a customized contract for you at a reasonable rate.

Cash versus Checks

Here's where you start determining what your payment policies are. Let's start with the king of all kings, cash. As a working makeup artist, cash is really the best, and the only secure way to go. In fact, many working makeup artists have decided to only accept cash. "Cash only" is part of their working policy. Outside of being the only form of payment without the chance of bouncing or deducting extra fees, it's instantly spendable. You don't have to rush to a bank to deposit it, wait for the credit in your merchant account, or transfer it online. It's yours to have and to hold.

But here's the problem: Who keeps cash on them anymore? I don't know about you, but if I actually have cash on hand, it's nothing short of a small miracle. I'm usually so short on cash that I'm the regular who pays for her meal off of the dollar menu with a debit card. Guilty as charged. And not only that, I'm a repeat offender. The simple truth is, people just don't use cash like they used to, so if you're planning on operating a cash-only business, you'll need to let your clients know in advance.

The next best thing to cash is a check. You can deposit it into your account without any fees, or cash it directly at the bank it was written from. The only problem here is the obvious one: What if it bounces or the check is no good? It's certainly a risk you take. You'll need to decide how you feel about personal checks and write your payment policies accordingly. Make sure to have several ways to contact a client in the event you should have to request another form of payment.

d.d.Nickel…makeup studio

123 Any Street~Anytown, USA

Bridal Contract

I, _____ , have hired d.d. Nickel to do _____ services at an agreed rate of $____ on the day of _____ at the address/location of _____ .

The bride and bridal party makeup is to be completed by _____ a.m./p.m.

There is a *$____ fee for each additional service added after the signing of this contract.

Please choose Option A or B (plus C, if you would like me to stay for touch-ups).

A. I have authorized d.d Nickel to charge the credit card number listed below 30 percent of the booked services in the event that I cancel her services at any time after the signing of this contract. I understand that if I DO NOT cancel, my credit card will not be charged and payment will be rendered in the full amount to d.d Nickel the day of the wedding by cash or personal check. If I choose to make full payment using the credit card listed below, my card will be charged in full no less than seven days prior to the wedding date listed above, with an additional processing fee of 5 percent.

Credit Card #_____exp._____ zip_____ security code_____

B. I have chosen not to submit a credit card as a deposit for the services listed above, but am leaving a deposit of 30 per-cent in cash or personal check. In the event that I wish to cancel, I agree that the deposit of 30 percent is nonrefund-able. I agree to pay the balance of the services the day of the wedding by either cash or personal check.

I am submitting/mailing a deposit:

In the amount of $_____ on the day of _____

Balance of: $ _____ Due: _____

C. d.d. Nickel will also stay on-site for makeup touch-ups, from _____ a.m./p.m., billed at an hourly rate of $100 p/h, for a total additional cost of $_____dollars.

Signature _____ Date_____

Contract may be e-mailed to: (e-mail address here)

Or mailed with a check to: 123 Any Street, Anytown, USA

*Please return the contract before _____ to secure the date. Contracts received after the contract expira-tion date above will be honored based on the date's availability.

Should You Accept Credit Cards?

You know, in a perfect world, we'd all be paying cash, but our new reality is that we all carry more plastic than the real green stuff. As I already confessed, I don't think twice about using my debit card to pay for a $1 iced tea and a $1 small fries. I think the answer here is yes, you need to have the ability to take debit and credit cards, especially if what you're charging for any particular service totals more than $100. Not only are credit cards more convenient for most people, but they also feel safer to carry. I don't know about you, but carrying more than $100 in my purse makes me a little uncomfortable. Although there is a fee for processing credit and debit cards, it's minimal compared to losing a sale or even deterring a client from booking an appointment with you because you don't take plastic. This is just part of doing business and accommodating the needs of all of your potential clients. In the end, this will bring you much more business than attracting just those who can pay cash.

The good news? Now it's easier than ever to process credit cards. You can open a merchant account and process credit cards through online services, lease a wireless credit card machine that you can take with you on the go, or even swipe and process cards from a small device on your iPhone or Android. You no longer have to have a storefront with lots of electrical equipment. Processing can be as mobile as you are.

The downside? There are costs involved that will decrease your profits, but as I mentioned before, those are relatively small when compared to the sales you'll potentially lose by not offering your client a variety of payment options. Your costs will vary based on the equipment and the type of merchant account or processing service you choose, but an investment in credit card processing is the only way, in my opinion, to run any kind of business in this day and age.

Here's an overview of some of your credit card processing options.

Traditional Processing

The traditional method of processing credit cards requires opening up a merchant account with a credit card processing company and then leasing or purchasing the credit machine from them. Their rates will vary, so it's important to shop around if this is the option that works best for you. Like many industries, there is a lot of competition, so you'll need to do your research in order to find the best value. This ultimately means there will be more money left in your pocket, so it's worth your time not to jump at the first offer you find.

You'll also want to look for a company that can offer you the type of equipment that works for you. There are a variety of options, but I'd recommend a wireless model that can go wherever you go, particularly if you don't have a home studio or storefront. The equipment can either be purchased outright or you can lease it for a monthly fee. (The latter means you'll be locked into a contract for a specific period of time, so keep that in mind. If someone comes along with a better offer, you may not be able to take advantage of it without losing money.)

Merchant Accounts for Mobile Devices

In my opinion, this is the best option for most of us. You can purchase a USB card swiper that attaches right to your mobile device (iPhone, Droid, iPad, PC or MAC laptop), allowing you to process credit cards with one swipe. It's fast, secure, and affordable. Unlike traditional processing, there are no contracts, minimums, or setup fees. You simply sign up for a merchant account, download the app onto your mobile device, and you're ready to go. You can swipe cards anytime, anywhere. Plus, the device is so small, it can go anywhere you and your phone go. Just like traditional processing, you'll want to shop around. There are deals that include free swipers and apps and some that charge a reasonable fee. Be sure to take note of the monthly fee, transaction fee, and discount rate (this is the amount you'll pay per transaction). These rates will vary by company.

PayPal

But wait. There's yet another option that will allow your clients to pay by credit or debit card, and that's using PayPal. You can process credit cards right from your computer without the need for additional equipment like a card swiper. There are two different ways you can get paid on PayPal.

- **Invoice the client:** PayPal allows you to e-mail invoices directly to your clients. They can then pay you and the funds will go directly into your PayPal account. You'll even receive a notification when the invoice has been paid. This works especially well when you're working with brides. You can invoice them their balance due well before the wedding day arrives.
- **Virtual terminal:** You can turn your computer into a credit card machine and process credit cards manually. You simply input all of the credit card information from your client and the funds are deposited directly into your PayPal account.

So PayPal is another affordable option. There are no monthly fees, setup fees, or cancellation fees for most PayPal standard merchant services. There will be a fee, however, for each transaction made, but the convenience of setup makes this a reasonable choice. The downside is, if you're on the move, you'll need to have a laptop with you. And I'm sure you're also wondering how you get your money out once the funds have been deposited into your PayPal account. The answer? You can simply transfer the funds from your PayPal account into your checking account, or you can apply for a PayPal debit card that you can use just like your regular bank card. Easy.

As you can see, there is a variety of options to suit everyone's needs. To start shopping for a credit card processing company, you can inquire at your local banks; most of them will have options for small businesses. Or you can do a simple Google search for "merchant account services" or "credit card processing for small businesses." Your search should direct you to reviews and comparisons of different companies and their offers. Like all banking and finance matters, rates and fees are always subject to change at any given moment—yet another reason to do some comprehensive research to find the right fit for you.

11

Just for Brides

When I first opened my makeup studio, I never intended to include brides in the business. I was working long hours on commercial jobs in New York City, and brides needed to book so far in advance. I just didn't think it was a good fit for me. I needed more flexibility in my schedule and couldn't commit to anything so far in advance. I would just offer lessons and sell makeup in my downtime. That was my plan. Besides, we'd all heard about the proverbial "bridezilla," and who wanted to be bothered with that? Until one day a friend called and said a work colleague's daughter was getting married in a week and the makeup artist they had booked canceled last minute, leaving them in a beauty lurch. Oh no! I happened to have the day free and accepted the offer to rescue the bride and bridal party from sure bridal beauty disaster, and what I found was, there was a lot of money to be made in bridal. Wow! I made as much (if not more) in those four hours than I would have on a full-day commercial job. It was close to home so there was no commute, and I left with cash in hand and a warm, fuzzy feeling, knowing I'd made someone feel beautiful on the biggest day of her life. What's not to like about making people feel good? So, bridal beauty it was. The timing was right to start promoting myself to the bridal market, so I started looking for ways to find more brides. I hit the Internet.

Attracting the Right Brides

While surfing the Internet, searching for ways to connect with more brides and get the bridal part of my business going, I started noticing that all brides and bridal markets aren't the same. There are as many types of brides as there are women. And there are all types of budgets. I had to figure out where I fit in before I could start attracting the right bride for my style of makeup, my philosophy on bridal beauty, and my price point. There were dozens of websites, all marketing to brides of every taste level and budget, and I had to narrow it down in order to find where I belonged. And believe me, I made a few mistakes along the way.

If you've decided to specialize in bridal beauty or start marketing yourself to the bridal industry, just as with other clients, you'll want to find the right brides for you. As we know, all brides and budgets are not created equally, so find your niche and market to that bride and the other wedding vendors that she might hire. When I first decided to include brides in my business, I searched the Internet high and low to find out what was happening in the world of bridal in my area and target markets. My intention was to service brides in Connecticut, near my studio, and in Vermont, where I also spend a lot of time. Through my research, I discovered that each market was vastly different. The bride was very different in both places, and I had to figure out how to market myself to each one. My rates were priced on the higher side for each market, so I clearly needed to find brides with bigger budgets and ones that would appreciate my experience as a seasoned makeup artist. It was clear I wasn't going to be working with every bride in the state, and that was okay. So where was she and how would I find her? I soon learned there are several ways to get started.

Bridal Portfolio

The first and most important thing to do is have an extensive portfolio of bridal work on your website or blog that she can see. Brides will be attracted to your work and portfolio and instantly find a connection with you. The more photos of real brides you have that appeal to your particular brides, the more success you'll have in attracting the right ones. You may choose to have before and after photos of brides that you've worked with, or photos from actual weddings that you acquired from past brides. You can also include any styled shoots you participated in.

And what do you do if you're just getting started and you don't have any photos of your bridal work? Well, believe it or not, this happened to me. I had years of experience in makeup, but my portfolio didn't have any photos of brides because my career didn't include bridal work at the time. It became clear to me as I was getting inquiries from brides that they wanted to see pictures of other brides—not models, not celebrities, but other women dressed up in white on their special day. So what does a makeup artist do? The obvious thing is, you need photos. If you don't have anything at all, you can choose to do snapshots of friends and family or brides that you're working with to get started. This is the most economical approach, but for the long term, a more professional presentation is the best way to go.

My best advice is to find a photographer in your area, preferably one who shoots a lot of weddings, and ask if they would be interested in collaborating with you to do some test shots. Be clear up front that you're new to bridal makeup, you're putting together your website and portfolio, and you'd love to partner with them to take a few bridal shots of your work. They may have a charge for their services, which in my mind is a good investment if you're building a quality website and portfolio, but many will offer their services for free. You may want to offer a link on your website's preferred vendor page, or write a nice blog post about them. Just be sure to include a photo credit and link to the photographer's website. This is really a win-win for both of you, so don't be shy about asking. You get to use the photos and the photographer gets their work in front of a new audience. However you decide to build your bridal portfolio, remember, brides want to see other brides, and if they see what they like, they'll call you. It's really that simple.

Power of Referrals

Another way to attract the right bride is to get a referral from another vendor that she's hired, like her venue, photographer, wedding planner, or florist. Makeup is usually one of the last priorities on the bride's extensive to-do list, and possibly one of the last services she books, so referrals can come from any number of places. When I first decided to get into bridal, I sent an e-mail to all of the wedding vendors I could find online who looked like a good match for my business and like they may potentially service my type of bride. I figured if I was attracted to their website, marketing approach, and portfolio of work, then my bride probably was too. I received a few direct e-mails back from vendors introducing themselves, and one planner even started sending me work right away.

The majority of my e-mail inquiries landed in cyberspace without a response, or so I thought. Several months later, I received an invitation to attend a networking party from a popular planner and met some quality wedding professionals who were more than happy to get to know me. They started sending me work right away. I even had one vendor, a videographer, send me an e-mail three years later. So you see, you never know where that introduction is going to land and what may become of it, so put yourself out there in front of the already-established wedding vendors. You can't go wrong by letting them know you're available for their brides.

And then there's marketing yourself online on the many bridal blogs and wedding directories. Like with all marketing efforts, try to find the blogs and directories that appeal to you, because they probably appeal to your bride too. In the beginning I signed up on every directory I could find that offered a reasonable package. I joined professional wedding organizations and signed up with a company that offered a comprehensive wedding marketing program, including participating in their wedding expos, listings in their free brochure, a database of brides to contact, and a listing on their website. In theory, it sounded like a great program, especially for someone just getting started, and I'm sure for many of their vendors, it was a good fit, but their bride just wasn't my bride. The program wasn't targeting the type of bride who was interested in me. The lesson is, the better you know who your bride is, the less trouble you'll have finding her. Today, I've narrowed down my marketing options and just advertise on one specific blog site that brings in traffic. Thankfully, most of my business comes from vendor referrals.

So, you think you're marketing to the right bride, you make contact, and she never books a trial with you. Don't take it personally. It's hard not to sometimes, especially when you're new and hungry for the work. She may admire your work but may not have the budget to hire you, and will look for someone who has a different pricing structure; or she may have contacted several artists she was interested in and decided to move forward with one of them. Just know, she wasn't the bride for you. If you're putting all of the right information out there, your bride will find you.

Booking the Bridal Trial

The bridal trial is an important part of the bridal beauty experience. It's a chance for you and the bride to meet, create a rapport about her wedding, and see if you are a match. It's your chance to create a makeup look that suits her wedding vision, personal style, and comfort level, and your opportunity to book a job. Most brides will request a trial before they book you for their wedding, so it's important to make sure you bring your A-game that day. You should think of it as a job interview.

So, how does a bridal trial work? Well, once the bride contacts you, she will most likely tell you she's interested in booking a trial run. Or if you feel your conversation with her is going well, then you could suggest that she come in for a trial. If you don't have a studio that you're working out of, then you'll want to meet the bride at the location of her choice, usually at her home.

If you've arranged to meet the bride at her home for the trial, be aware that there are sometimes a few challenges. The biggest one for me is lighting. Ask her to set up near a window that has plenty of natural light, and if she has a barstool to sit on. The majority of brides will lead you to their kitchen table or bathroom for the trial. Regular dining chairs are often too low to work comfortably and for you to see your work properly, so you may consider keeping a director's chair or barstool in your car so you'll have a taller chair, just in case. My director's chair has come in handy many, many times.

The second consideration is mirrors. Handheld mirrors are great, and you should have one with you, but they're too small for the bride to make a true assessment of the look. Most people have mirrors around the house, but they may be in dimly lit spaces and may not show off the look you've created in the right way. Encourage the bride to look at her makeup in a variety of mirrors and lighting situations. Even when I work with a bride in my studio, I have her look in several different mirrors, and then we go outside with the handheld mirror to see the makeup in natural light. She's always surprised when we go outside and see how different the makeup looks in completely natural light as opposed to overhead or lamp lighting. In many cases, it's been the outdoor lighting that's made her fall in love with her look and hire me on the spot. That's why starting the trial in as close to natural lighting as you can is key. And remind your bride that her wedding day will be a long and glorious day, filled with many different lighting situations. Most weddings will start in the afternoon and continue well into the evening, so looking at her makeup in several lighting situations will more closely represent how she'll look throughout her wedding day.

Another consideration is distractions. Kids, dogs, fiancés, the television, and the telephone can all be challenges in keeping your potential bride relaxed and excited about the makeup trial. I did a trial not too long ago at the bride's home and it was a difficult one. The contractors were in the next room stripping the floors, her fiancé kept coming into the room to ask questions, the television was on full blast with a morning talk show, and her two dogs kept vying for her undivided attention. Clearly it would be hard to focus on the task at hand, which was creating the perfect makeup look for her wedding, only a month away. The good news is, after some struggles, we got through it, created a look she loved and she booked me for her wedding, but be aware that keeping the bride focused is something to consider when you're working out of their home.

And lastly, how do you charge for the trial? Well, just like pricing every other service, you should come up with pricing that is competitive and reasonable for your area. Take a look at what other artists are charging, and again, figure out where you fit in. Because it's a trial or test run, your pricing should be competitive enough so that potential brides will be interested in booking with you. Pricing yourself too high for the trial could discourage brides from even considering you. Also, keep in mind that a trial is just that—a test—so if the bride decides not to book you for her wedding, you want to make sure you're being compensated for your time during the trial. You can consider offering the trial for free or at a discounted rate if the bride books you for her wedding day.

Offering Extras

We've talked about offering extras before, but what can you do specifically for a bride? Sometimes offering something extra will make the difference between booking the job or not. Here are some ideas:

- Offer a free bridal trial to encourage them to book you.

- Offer discounts to large bridal parties: the more people they book, the less they pay per person.

- Many makeup artists charge travel fees. Consider waiving the travel fee for larger bridal parties.

- Some artists charge extra for false lashes. Offer lashes as part of your package price to anyone in the bridal party who would like them.

- If you are also selling makeup as part of your business, offer the bride a lipstick or lip gloss of her choice and blotting papers as a complimentary part of your package. She'll appreciate having products to touch up with during the day.

- Offer a free or discounted makeup lesson to the bride and her bridal party after the wedding so they can enjoy learning all of the tricks and tips you used for the wedding. If you sell makeup, she may want to purchase the products you used on her. This may also encourage a bride to become a regular client.

These are just a few ideas. Research what the other artists in your area are offering and come up with packages and incentives that will work for your type of bride.

The Bridal Trial Experience

Now that you've booked the trial and met the bride, how do you get the trial started? Very simply, ask a lot of questions. You certainly don't want to barrage or bombard her with questions—you're not an FBI interrogator—but the more information you have about her wedding and her personal makeup style, the easier it will be for you to create a winning makeup look. I always ask about the venue first. Will she be getting married in a church ceremony or on the beach? Would she consider her wedding formal, traditional, or casual? Knowing where she's getting married may give you a clue about what the mood of the wedding will be. It may be a casual, sand-in-the-toes kind of wedding, or she may be getting married in a formal mansion. Whatever the case may be, you have to start by asking questions.

Next, ask about her dress. What does it look like? Is it Cinderella or Old Hollywood, vintage or modern, lace or chiffon? You get the idea. You can even ask the bride to bring a photo of her dress to the trial. I find this extremely helpful, and most brides will have a photo handy, either from a magazine or the Internet. What colors has she chosen for her big day? Bright, cheery colors, autumnal colors, or beach shades? All this gives you an idea of who she is and what she's envisioning for her wedding. Does she have an idea of what she'd like to do with her hair? The hair always complements the makeup, so asking this may also give you some information about where she'd like to go with makeup. And, of course, ask her if she has anything specific in mind for makeup.

I always request when I'm booking the trial that the bride look through magazines or online for looks that she likes, or doesn't like. I'm a visual person, and having a visual of what she likes helps immensely in figuring out where to start. Brides may say they want a "natural" look or a "smoky" eye, but there is so much interpretation in those words, it's sometimes difficult to know where her comfort level is. One girl's smoky eye is another girl's natural look. Lastly, ask what she would do if she were doing her own makeup for a big night out. Would she use primarily neutral colors, or is she comfortable wearing color? Does she wear foundation or just powder? Does she wear eyeliner? Does she like color on her lips or does she prefer something neutral? How would she normally do her eyes? This is where you'll get the most information about her comfort level with color. You may even consider asking to see her personal makeup collection and asking to see which colors she wears the most.

Once you've had a chance to chat about the particulars of her wedding and gotten to know more about her, it's time to start the trial. After gathering all of the information about her, you should have an idea where you want to go with her makeup. I always start with the basics, primer and foundation, and then pull out a selection of colors that I think would look great on her and suit her particular style. I like to ask if any of the colors jump out at her and if she has a preference on where to start. Many brides will come to you with a clear vision of how they want to look, and that's great—this makes it easier for you—but many will come to you looking for advice and suggestions. They won't have any idea at all, either because they don't normally wear makeup and don't have any experience with it, or because it's not a high priority. They just know they want to look "a little better than normal" for the big day.

If your bride does have strong opinions on her makeup, then start with her preferred look. If you think the look she's chosen isn't appropriate for her, then you might suggest doing what she'd like on one side of her face and trying another look on the other side. Sometimes the look a bride has chosen has come from a magazine or is a duplicate of a celebrity look. It's great to try those looks, but remind them that many times the looks you see in print and on TV are very dramatic in person and may not be the best choice for your wedding day. Find a way to balance the look she desires with what is appropriate for a wedding. If your bride has no idea what she'd like for makeup, I usually do the same thing: choose a few colors and start with one look on one side and one look on the other. The great thing is, if she's uncomfortable with what you've done, you can always try something new or make adjustments up or down.

After you've completed her look, write everything down on a face chart or form you create. I don't know about you, but even though my memory is pretty good, I can't remember what colors I used on every single bride, especially if I met with them a year or so in advance. I write down all the colors and products I used in the final look, and also make some notes about the bride, like the details of her big day, including location, how many are in her bridal party, where they will be getting ready (because sometimes that location is different than the actual wedding location), her personal contact information, including mailing address, cell-phone number, and e-mail address. I also like to know how she was referred to me (online or from another vendor) and what other wedding vendors she's hired. This is essentially your cheat sheet so you can duplicate the exact look for her on her wedding day. Include as much information as you need to successfully re-create the look. And what if the bride doesn't book you on the spot? Put together a chart anyway. You never know if she's going to call back and want to hire you, so you'll want to be prepared.

Name:_____ Trial Date: _____

Face

Pressed Foundation	$40.00	____ _____
Liquid Foundation	$40.00	_____
Sheer Tint	$40.00	_____
Concealer	$22.00	_____

Eyes

Gel Liner	$20.00			_____
Eye Shadow	$20.00			_____
Brow Powder	$16.00			_____
Lashes	none	demi	full	

Cheek

Blush (cream or powder)	$22.00	_____

Lips

Lip Liner	$18.00	_____
Liquid Lips	$20.00	_____
Gloss	$20.00	_____
Long-Wear Lipstick	$22.00	_____

Wedding Details

Wedding Date: _____

Number of people for makeup: _____

Address (where you're getting ready): _____

What time do you want to be finished with makeup?: _____ a.m./p.m.

How did you hear about d.d.Nickel? _____

Name of your photographer: _____

Name of your hair stylist: _____

Please list other important vendors (venue, florist, caterer, etc.): _____

_____

_____

Contact Information

Your Contact Info: _____

Mailing Address: _____

E-mail: _____

Cell: _____ Other Phone: _____

Contract Dated: _____ Contract Expires: _____

Many brides will ask if they can bring their friend, sister, or mother with them to the trial. The answer should be yes! They'll feel more comfortable having someone with them that they trust, and it's nice to have another objective opinion. Sometimes it's hard for women to see themselves in a different way, and having feedback from their loved one is often good encouragement. You may ask your brides to wear white or ivory to their trial so they'll have that color next to their face when you're working. It will be more representative of how the makeup will look once she's dolled up in her gown. And scheduling her hair trial the same day is also a good idea. I find that if a bride comes in with her casual street clothes on, and her hair is undone, it's hard to know how the makeup will look once her full look comes together.

Many brides will also want to take photos of the makeup when they are at the trial. I have mixed feelings about this. I understand that they want to see how the makeup will look in pictures, but snapping a photo on your phone or on your mother's point-and-shoot won't represent how the makeup will look in professional wedding photos. Snapshots are just that, and the application I provide always takes into consideration how the makeup will look when photos are taken by a professional photographer. If she loves her makeup in the snapshot, then you have nothing to worry about. If she has some objections, do what you can to address them and tweak the look to her liking, while gently reminding her that the makeup look you've created is meant to ensure that she's camera-ready for the big day.

Securing the Date

The trial is complete. You've created her wedding-day look based on your conversations with her, and you've done your best to put together a look she'll love. So, how do you know if you're hired? How do you secure the date? My experience has been that most brides will let you know at the end of the trial if they are interested in securing the date with you. They'll double-check your availability and ask if they can book you for the day. Other brides will pay for their trial, say a polite thank-you, and go about their day; you may or may not hear back from them. Both scenarios are fine. Of course, you did your best for her and you're eager to book the job, but don't be offended if someone doesn't hire you right off the bat. Some brides may leave and not book you until they've had a chance to meet with other makeup artists. Some book trials with several people until they find the perfect fit. Some may need more time to show the makeup you did for them to friends and family before deciding, or they may want to wear the makeup around for the day to see how well it will last. Some will call you back and book you, and some will not. Do you hard-sell them at the end of the trial? Well, that's up to you. Each artist will have her own way of working with clients. I'm more of a soft-sell kind of girl. I'd prefer for my work to sell itself. I want only the clients that love and appreciate the work I've done for them, so if they're unsure, we may not be a great match. I don't want someone hiring me because they feel pressured. Whatever your approach is to securing the date, do your best work, be confident in your skills as an artist, and the right brides (for you) will book you.

You're Hired!

The bride booked you. Yippee! Now you want to make sure to get it all in writing. Have her sign a contract (see chapter 10 for details). It may sound like a hassle, but it secures the date for you and gives the bride reassurance that you'll be there for her on her big day. It's customary within the wedding industry to secure the date with a contract, and most wedding vendors require one. Because brides book so far in advance, it's a measure of security for you and her. You'll find as your business grows that brides may be booking you a year or so in advance, sometimes before they've even had a trial if they love your work, so make sure you have the date, rate, and number of people confirmed in a contract.

Early on, I didn't have a contract. There were never contracts in my commercial work, so it never occurred to me that I would need one just for a bride. If I said I would be there, I would be there, period, but I learned early on that everyone's commitment to their word isn't the same. On more than one occasion, I had brides ask to book me, I sent them a contract to secure the date, and then never heard from them again. I now give brides two weeks to return the contract, and I hold the date for that two-week period. If I haven't received the contract within that time period, I open the date back up and will schedule her in later only if there is still availability. You can decide how your contract will read and what your specific policies are, but my experience has taught me that it's better to have every detail in writing.

In addition to a contract, it's customary to request a deposit to hold the date. The amount of the deposit varies by artist and their particular policies, but I've found that when someone commits to you with money, she is less likely to cancel or look for someone else. It's just a sign of good faith that she wants to hire you. Money plus the contract seals the deal. You determine what your deposit amount is. I offer two options. One is a credit card hold, just like a hotel. I hold the card number and details and only charge the card if they cancel. They can then pay me in full the day of the wedding by cash or check. Some people are uncomfortable leaving their credit card details with a stranger, and that's understandable, but this has turned out to be the most popular form of securing the date. Weddings are so expensive and there are so many up-front expenses that it's a nice option to pay later. Of course, this only works if you accept credit cards. My second option is to put a percentage down on the total amount due. Some artists just ask for a flat rate from all brides as a deposit, no matter how many are in their bridal party. You decide what works for you, but get a signed contract and a deposit that makes you comfortable before you secure the day and turn down other potential brides for that date.

Scheduling Day of Timelines

You've booked a happy bride. She signed the contract and happily secured your time with a deposit, and the big day is drawing near. Let's say she booked you for a total of six people: the bride, her mother, mother-in-law, and three bridesmaids. How much time will you need to get the job done? There's nothing worse than a makeup artist holding up the wedding proceedings because the makeup isn't done in time. You have to know how long it takes for you to do makeup on one person and then calculate in a little wiggle room or cushion.

Wedding days are chaotic, hectic, and can be stressful for the bride if things aren't working out as she planned. Part of your job is to make sure her time with you on the big day is a pleasant experience. Even if other things are going wrong, you want to know that it isn't you. Carefully assess how long it really takes you to do a face. If you're new and not sure, practice on a friend and time yourself. In general, newer artists who are less confident in their skills are slower. If that's you and it takes you an hour or so to do one person, be up-front with the bride and let her know you'll need to schedule an hour per person. You want to make sure you've scheduled in enough time, not only to get the job done, but to do it well. Brides will talk about the experiences they had with you and you want the reviews to be positive. Be sure you leave the bride with good feelings about your professionalism and ability to fulfill her beauty needs that day. I schedule thirty minutes per person, but I've been doing this for a long time, and am confident in my ability to get the job done in that time frame. Let your time clock be your guide.

Once you know how much time you need, there are a few other things to consider when putting together a beauty timeline for the day, such as how are the rest of her wedding vendors scheduled? For example, the bride may be getting married at 5:00 p.m., but her photographer may have requested time to do portraits and family photos before the ceremony, so she may need to be ready and at her venue by 2:00 p.m. Or the hair stylist she hired is only available to do hair in the morning, and she'd like to do hair and makeup at the same time. Also, what you really need to know is, what time does she want to be ready to get dressed? I always recommend that brides allow thirty minutes to get dressed before heading out the door. Make sure you cover all of these things with her as you're nailing down the timeline for the day. If you're working directly with a wedding planner instead of the bride, make sure she or he knows how much time you will need with each person so they can schedule you in accordingly.

Be on Time

It should go without saying (and pains me to even have to write about this): Be on time. It seems so simple, and yet so many artists I've known are chronically late. If you're someone who is always running late, keep in mind that keeping a bride waiting means she may not have time for all of the services she's booked with you. If you're thirty minutes late, that might mean one of the bridesmaids may not get her makeup done, and most of all, it means you'll leave the bride with a negative impression of you and your business. If you can't complete everyone's makeup in time, you may also have to refund some of the money, so it's best to be prompt, professional, and ready to go at the planned time. Of course, things come up, like traffic accidents, and not all situations can be controlled, so always have the phone number of the bride and someone in her bridal party handy. Call them immediately if you feel like you may be running late.

If you're headed to a location you've never been to before, which happens quite often, and are unsure where you're going, build in some extra time to get there. I often use Google Maps or MapQuest to find directions and the timing is rarely accurate. Get an estimate of how long it will take you to get there, including traffic, and build in a little time for safety. I'd always rather be early than late.

The Bride, the Bridal Party, and the Big Day

In most cases, you've already met the bride, but most likely you haven't met her bridal party. That means you're going in cold and doing makeup on a group of women you've never met before. This can be daunting if you're inexperienced. Since you don't know what everyone looks like, be sure to have your full kit with you, and be prepared for every age and skin tone. You're the Girl Scout of Beauty, always prepared and ready for any beauty emergency, the one who guarantees that everyone will be looking the best she's ever looked. As you're starting each person's makeup, greet her warmly, ask her name, and always bring a smile to the day. Remember, this is the bride's big day, and she is relying on you to not only make everyone look her best, but also to be a fun addition to the getting-ready process. She probably hired you not only for your makeup work, but also for your personality, so come ready to shine. Keep your troubles at home, and show up with a positive attitude and friendly personality; you never know who you may meet. One of the bridesmaids may be getting married soon and in need of a makeup artist, or the mother of the bride may want to book a makeup lesson down the road.

Makeup for Mothers and Bridesmaids

Before you even start the makeup, try to establish beforehand whether the bride has any special requests or directions for the bridal party's makeup. Most brides won't have an opinion on this, but it's better to know her preferences going into the situation. Does she want everyone to look the same, or is she open to what works best on each person? What are the colors the bridesmaids will be wearing? If there is no direction for the day, I usually ask each bridal party member if she has anything in particular in mind for makeup, and go from there. Each person has her own individual style, so take that into consideration when creating a cohesive look for the group.

As an example, I had a bride who at her bridal trial didn't have any direction for the bridal party, or for her mother. As I was getting everyone ready, it was time for her mom to have her makeup done. Her mother was on the elderly side, and quite clearly stated that she wanted a "smoky eye." I would never have recommended a smoky eye for her, but she was insistent, so that's what I did. Mom was thrilled with her look for the day and couldn't stop raving about it. The bride, on the other hand, was very unhappy, and wanted me to change it. In the end, Mom won, as moms sometimes do. Consider this a cautionary tale: Always ask if the bride has any special requests for the rest of her bridal party.

Create a Relaxing Environment

Once you're there and you've settled in and set up, it's time to get to work. Every bride's day will be different, and you never know what you're walking into until you get there. It can be a stressful, chaotic day depending on those around her, or it can be a joyous day, full of love and fun. We've all heard of bridezillas, and no one wants to service one of those for the day, but part of what separates a good artist from a great one is their ability to adjust and adapt to any situation around her. You have to be able to read the mood of the room and fit in. You're a chameleon. Does the bride prefer to be quiet that day? If so, incessant chatting will just stress her out. Is she a party girl having a fun time with her friends? Then they may want you to join in the laughter. Whatever the mood is, your job is to create as much of a relaxing environment as possible, and to not contribute to anything negative that may be going on. Keep it light.

Staying On Time and On Track

Because it's such a hectic, busy day and any number of things can go wrong, how do you stay on track and keep the makeup moving, so to speak? In a perfect world, ask the bride to supply you with a schedule of who will be coming and going at what time, or make one of your own when you arrive. This helps keep everyone on track so each bridal party member knows where she needs to be at what time. If you don't have a schedule from the bride, ask if everyone who is having her makeup done can be in the room together, so as you finish one person, there is someone there waiting to be next. Use this "Wedding Day Schedule" to help keep you on track.

Following Up: Getting Reviews, Testimonials, and Images

I often leave a bride and her bridal party and wonder how they felt about their experience. Once the big day is over, I may never hear from them again. For out-of-town brides, it's often out of sight, out of mind, but it's important to obtain feedback from as many brides as possible. Getting reviews and testimonials from happy brides is one of the best tools for booking new brides. Brides like to hear from other happy brides. When I first started approaching the bridal market, in addition to not having many photos of brides, I also didn't have any testimonials—not because my bridal work was bad, but because I just didn't have any. I started getting inquiries from potential brides asking to see photos and testimonials or references. What's a makeup artist to do?

Date: _____

Bride's name: _____

Bride's contact information (day of wedding phone number/e-mail):

_____

Location address (where you'll be doing makeup):

_____

Number of makeup services booked (including bride): _____

Arrival time (what time you need to be there to set up): _____

Start time (the first makeup application): _____

Name of hair stylist (if applicable): _____

Hair stylist contact information: _____

Arrival time of the hair stylist: _____

Name of photographer (if applicable): _____

Photographer contact information: _____

Arrival time of the photographer: _____

Create a schedule below for each person based on the amount of time you need:

Start Time	Name	Completed	Paid
_____	_____	❏	❏
_____	_____	❏	❏
_____	_____	❏	❏
_____	_____	❏	❏
_____	_____	❏	❏
_____	_____	❏	❏
_____	_____	❏	❏
_____	_____	❏	❏
_____	_____	❏	❏
_____	_____	❏	❏

Deposit paid: _____   Balance due: _____

One of the first things you can do is follow up with the bride several weeks later, after she's had a chance to settle into married life, and ask her if she had a good experience with you. If so, ask if she would be willing to write a testimonial. This is obviously a very direct approach and may work for some of you, while others will be uncomfortable; still, it's something to consider. Many brides, once they've settled in, will send a card or e-mail thanking you for your time and services. I've amassed a collection of notes sent from happy brides that I proudly display in my studio.

There are also free websites that will allow brides to review your services online. One of them is called WeddingWire, and is powered by Martha Stewart. It's free and it links to many other sites, so your reviews will be seen in multiple places online. You can send your brides an e-mail invitation to review you. As we discussed earlier, the review is based on five categories: Quality of Service, Responsiveness, Professionalism, Value, and Flexibility. Many brides are already familiar with WeddingWire and may have searched for vendors there. Some will voluntarily write reviews of their vendors after the wedding, so signing up on the site is a great tool. Hopefully, you've done a tremendous job and your reviews are stellar, but if not, don't fret. WeddingWire also gives you, the vendor, an opportunity to respond. I've seen responses to bad reviews that were less than flattering to the vendor, so even though your feelings may be hurt, try to respond to negative reviews in a positive, professional way. I think every bride searching for vendors knows that no vendor is perfect, and some brides just can't be pleased, so if the majority of your reviews are glowing, a bride is still likely to get in touch with you if she loves your work.

Another way to get reviews and testimonials is from other wedding vendors. Wedding planners, photographers, and other vendors you've worked with on a wedding may also agree to write a review for you. On WeddingWire, you can also get what they call "endorsements" from vendors that you've worked with who appreciate your work, and you can "endorse" them in return.

Also consider adding your reviews to your website. I have a page dedicated on my blog just for reviews and testimonials. Adding these glowing remarks to your site for potential brides to see when they are searching for an artist may be one of the reasons they get in touch. I include both bride and vendor testimonials on my page.

And you simply must get photos from the weddings you've worked on. You already know this: Brides want to see your work. So how do you get photos of the brides you've worked with? Some photographers in the wedding industry make it a point to send all of the vendors they worked with images of the wedding you worked on together. They will usually send you a disc or e-mail the photos for download in an online-gallery format. It's a great way for them to get their work and their name out there, and goes a long way toward goodwill with other vendors in the industry. On the bridal form I use at the bridal trial, I ask the bride to supply the name of her photographer and other vendors so I can contact them for photos if I need to. Unfortunately, some photographers aren't as generous and may not think to send you images on their own, but it's certainly fine for you to contact them and request some photos. I would suggest this, especially if you're still trying to build your portfolio. Some brides may even send you a photo or two in an e-mail or in a card.

Once you do have photos of past weddings, be aware that each photographer has copyrights to those photos. Find out if they have any restrictions on the use of the photos. For example, I had a bride that didn't want photos of her wedding posted on the photographer's blog, so they weren't able to post them. The photographers were still kind enough to send me a disc of images, but I never posted the photos on my site either. There may also be restrictions on how the images can be used on social media sites, like Facebook and Twitter. In any case, ask the photographer how the photos can be used and always credit him when using the photos, both online and in print.

Converting Brides into Regular Clients

When you think about how many women you meet when you're working with brides, it's just common sense to encourage all of those women to become regular clients. You want them to think of you not only as the makeup artist that did their makeup for their wedding, but the person they think of first when they think about makeup. All of these women have other occasions outside of weddings, and many of them will want to have their makeup done. You don't want them to head to the local department store when they go out on a Friday night, or when they have a special event or gala; you want them to think of you, and you only. If you also sell makeup as part of your business, then you want them to call you first when they need a new lipstick or want to change their look for the season.

When you're working at a wedding, be sure to have your business cards or brochures out so everyone can take one. I have found that even though they may be getting ready for a wedding, most women will ask you for makeup tips or what your favorite products are. That's a great time to mention the other services you offer, whether it's makeup lessons, personal makeup shopping services, or products that you sell. You may even want to offer specials to the bridal party or think of other incentives to encourage them to call you again. Ask them to sign your guest book with their e-mail address, and put them on your e-mail list for newsletter updates. Whatever it is, be creative and turn those brides into regular clients.

Wedding Industry Developments

A new development in the bridal market is emerging, and it's the legalization of same-sex marriages. For you as a makeup artist, and any vendor servicing the bridal industry, that means that the number of people interested in employing your services for their wedding just increased significantly. As more people are allowed to wed, there's more opportunity for you. You may be thinking that just same-sex female couples would be interested in makeup, but when I started my bridal business in Connecticut, the state had just legalized same-sex marriage. A good friend of mine was marrying his partner of many years. The grooms hired me to make sure their family members, including their sisters and moms, looked their best on the day of the wedding. To find out more about same-sex wedding traditions and considerations, you can visit www.gayweddinginstitute.com. This site specializes in same-sex unions and offers training to wedding vendors looking to reach out to same-sex couples.

Currently many states recognize same-sex marriage, so check your local laws to find out if you live in one of these areas. Many countries outside of the United States also recognize same-sex marriages. If you live in one of these areas, you may consider learning more about the traditions and customs that are unique to same-sex couples.

12

Expanding your Business

So, your new life and career as a makeup artist has started to take off. You have a regular roster of clients, and you're driving to and fro, making all of them look their very best. But you've been thinking, it would be nice to actually have a place of your own, a home base. How do you know when it's time to take the big leap and expand? Well, that's a very personal decision, and will be different for everyone. Expansion will mean different things to different people. Let's look at a few possibilities.

Opening a Studio or Storefront

This is certainly a big leap and a big expense if you've been working from your home. Whether you've been meeting clients at their location or you've been meeting with them in your home, opening a studio or storefront may be the next step in growing your business. Certainly one of the biggest considerations will be money. It will cost significantly more to operate a storefront or studio that's not connected to your home. You'll obviously have added expenses. Here are a few you'll want to consider before making the leap.

- **Deposit:** If you're interested in renting a space, there is generally a deposit required. That amount will be dictated by the landlord and the laws in your state.
- **Monthly rent:** There will obviously be a monthly payment for rent. It goes without saying that you'll want to be sure to find a space that fits comfortably into your budget.
- **Utilities:** You'll need to pay for utilities, including electricity, heat, phone, and/or computer service. Get an estimate from the utility companies on the average usage of the space you're considering.

- **Renovations:** Depending on the space you choose, you may need to update it with lighting, mirrors, paint, and flooring. You may also need to make some physical changes to the space to make it functional. Most commercial landlords will negotiate, and will often include some repairs and renovations as part of the lease agreement, at no charge to you. It never hurts to ask.
- **Furniture and decor:** Obviously you'll want to personalize your space and make it your own. Your costs will depend on the size of the space and your taste and personal style.
- **Equipment:** Equipment expenses can include computer and phone systems, credit card machines, TV or audio/visual equipment.

As you can see, it's no small undertaking and the expenses can add up quickly, so you'll want to carefully weigh the pros and cons. For me, the pros were the ability to meet clients in my own space, where I was comfortable and could control everything from the lighting to the music. By having my own space, I'm not subject to doing makeup in spaces with dim lighting or fighting the chaos of someone else's home. I've created an environment where I'm relaxed and the client is comfortable before she ever sits in the makeup chair.

Did You Know?

The precursor to the contemporary makeup studio was called an "enameling studio," and was found in big cities, like New York City, in the 1800s into the early 1900s. These studios were frequented by women living on the extreme sides of society—courtesans, dancing girls, and women of ill repute—and on the other side of the coin, royalty. A patron could have her face painted into a mask that would last, depending on how much she paid, for up to a year.

The face was examined and hair was removed with liniment or plaster. The "enameler" would fill in the wrinkles and lines with a plastic or yielding paste, and then the face and bust were coated with a paste made from arsenic, white lead, and other ingredients. The look was finished with rouge. You could also have your hands powdered white, brighten your eyes with prussic acid, and enhance your veins by painting them blue, all in vogue for the day.

If you're not sure you're ready to manage a place of your own, but would still like to have a space to call your own, you might consider renting a corner or a chair in a local hair salon, nail salon, clothing boutique, or skin-care center. Sharing the responsibility and expense of a place just might be the right solution for you. If you do decide it's time to jump right in and open a makeup studio or storefront, my best advice is to do your homework, crunch the numbers, and move forward with confidence. It was the best decision I ever made, and just might be the right decision for you too.

Hiring and Training Assistants

No man is an island, and sometimes to move forward and grow, you need a little help. You may need a personal assistant to handle the phone calls, inquiries, e-mails, and correspondence. Or you may find you need someone to help promote you, someone who can expertly navigate the world of social media and marketing. Or you may have more makeup inquiries than you can handle and want to hire and train other makeup artists. Whatever your needs are, hiring and training team members may be the next step.

When making the decision to hire someone, you have to first decide if you're ready to be a manager. Hiring and training assistants takes time and the ability to lead and inspire. Some people are natural leaders and comfortable in that role, and others are not. Assess your desire to be both a makeup artist and a manager before you take others on your journey with you.

Okay, so you're going to go for it. You know you have the qualities and the time to lead a team. What qualities do you look for when you're hiring, and how do you decide who will be a good fit? When there are only a few people on a team, you want to make sure that everyone is a team player and that their personalities will complement each other. The last thing you need is to find out that your team members were out in the field on a job and there was a conflict in front of the client. Here are the steps I would follow to try to find the right match:

- **Résumé:** This is an obvious step, but because makeup artistry is subjective and may not be everyone's first career, I ask to see a résumé just to get an idea of background and level of dedication in past or current jobs. If they have a background in makeup, that's obviously a plus, but many are looking just to assist in addition to another full-time career.

- **References:** Again, because this is a nontraditional industry, the candidate may not have references directly related to makeup artistry, but past employers will be able to give you feedback on punctuality, dedication to following through, and other qualities that also apply in makeup artistry.
- **Portfolio:** This is big. Ask to see a portfolio, either online or a hard copy, or if they don't have a professional portfolio, snapshots of their work. Keep in mind that many photos will be retouched by the photographer, so it's sometimes hard to assess the talent of the artist; nonetheless, it's a good place to start.
- **Makeup demonstration:** I like to see a potential artist's work in person. This is the only real way you can assess her work. Ask her to bring in a model and have her do a makeup demo for you. You can dictate the look or looks you'd like her to do.
- **Interview:** There's no replacement for a good old conversation. You'll want to find out what excites them about doing makeup, how they got started, what kind of training they have, if any, and what their personal and professional goals are.

After you have all of the information you need, it just comes down to a gut feeling: Are you compatible, and do you connect? Do you think they will take direction well, and are they eager for some training? Are they trustworthy and someone you feel can represent you and your brand?

Once you've found the right person, then what? Well, you'll need to make sure they're well trained to represent you in makeup artistry and that they have the skills necessary to successfully service your clients' needs. You'll want to spend time making sure they are trained, not only in your signature or preferred makeup techniques, but also in customer service and client relations. Taking the extra time to build their confidence and skill level before they meet with clients on their own will build trust between you and them, and ensure your clients always have a positive experience, no matter who is working with them.

Offering Other Beauty Services

Some things just go hand in hand, like peanut butter and jelly, Bert and Ernie, and Donny and Marie. You just can't say one without the other. Makeup also has companions, and one just won't look as good without the other. Good skin, a great haircut, perfect brows. These things all complete the picture, and if one of them is off, the makeup just won't have the impact that it should. So, how do you help your client complete her look well past the makeup application? Well, there are two ways. You can obviously recommend professionals that you trust in each area—I have a roster of pros that I send clients to—or you can consider offering these services in your new space. The more you have to offer your client, the more likely she is to come and see you on a regular basis. Now, I'm not a licensed hair stylist or aesthetician, but if you have been to cosmetology school and are able to provide other services to your client, you might want to add those things to your menu of services. Not only will it be convenient for your client to get several services in one location, but it will also mean repeat business for you. The more opportunity they have to come and see you, the better. If you have a new space and you're not trained in any other services, consider sharing your space with other professionals. You'll have the same benefit of repeat business, but you'll gain new business by sharing clients.

Here are a few ideas of other services you could offer:

- **Hair styling:** This is a no-brainer. The best makeup application in the world just won't look as good if someone is in dire need of a new haircut and color. I see it all the time: overgrown roots, frayed ends, and hair without any kind of shape. A limp, lifeless mop. Your hair frames your face, so you'll want to have a hair professional to recommend, or even to invite into your new space. If you don't want to have a stylist as a permanent fixture, consider offering monthly hair-styling seminars or "Beauty and Blow-Out Nights."
- **Brows:** Brow shaping is another important service to offer. Brows frame the eyes and are going to highlight the makeup that you apply. A well-groomed brow opens up the eye and makes the face look brighter. If you're trained in waxing, threading, or tweezing, consider offering brow shaping as one of your services. It will generate repeat business because brows require regular upkeep.
- **Lash extensions:** What girl doesn't want long, luscious lashes? It opens up the eye and can make someone look more youthful. Offering lash extensions is also another way to bring in regular business because they require regular maintenance. With a simple Google search, you can find professional training and certification directly from the lash extension suppliers.
- **Skin care:** If you've already been doing makeup, chances are you've encountered a client with bad skin. And you know as well as I do that no matter

how good you are at makeup, applying it over bad skin can just make the client look worse. You just can't cover it up. Encouraging healthy, clear skin is the one way to ensure that your makeup application looks perfect every time. The better the skin, the better the makeup will look.

- **Nails:** Now, I'm a girlie girl, as I suspect you are too, and there's nothing I enjoy more than a manicure-pedicure. For some reason, it just makes me feel more human. Although your fingers and toes don't necessarily have a direct impact on your face, it is a nice complement to a well-groomed package.
- **Massage:** Massage is another service that many women enjoy and schedule regularly. Invite a licensed massage therapist to use your space to service your clients.
- **Accessories:** What girl doesn't like a little bling or want to treat herself to something special now and then? Offering cosmetic bags, candles, jewelry, or other items as add-ons can boost your revenue. Consider seeking out local artists or unique, handmade items to feature in your space.

Whether you decide to offer any extra services beyond makeup is a personal choice, but either way, be sure to have a list of professionals handy whom you trust and feel confident in recommending. Your client will appreciate you leading her in the right direction, and you'll build a valuable relationship with another beauty professional. Priceless.

Selling Retail

Okay, you've been working hard, you've perfected your techniques, gained a clientele, and even opened up a space where you can dedicate all of your energy as a professional makeup artist, but you're tired of selling everyone else's products. You're recommending product after product, sending your clients to the department store with list after list. It's time to find a way to have products ready for your clients when they need them. But how much does it cost to carry a line of makeup? Well, that can vary, but there are many ways, in a variety of price points, to supply your clients with quality products that you love and think will meet their needs. Selling products directly to your clients also has the long-term benefit of recurring business. They'll come back to you to restock their products when the time comes.

Depending on your budget and level of commitment to selling product, there are several options. We'll look first at companies you're already familiar with. Known as

"Direct Sellers," you or some of your clients may already be using some of their products. Becoming a direct sales representative for one or more of these companies may be a great way for you to have product to sell, earn some income, and not make an enormous monetary investment to get started. These companies also offer training on their products and support, such as a personalized website, so your clients can easily order products. They also vigorously market the products for you. Here are a few of the top direct sales cosmetics companies you may be interested in exploring.

- **Avon (www.avon.com):** We're all familiar with the proverbial "Avon Lady," but Avon has become the largest direct seller of cosmetics in the world. It's a recognizable brand and one your clients may already be comfortable with. You can get started with Avon as a representative for little more than the cost of a lipstick.
- **Mark (www.meetmark.com):** Mark is a line of cosmetics and products targeted toward the young and trendy shopper. If your clientele is hip and on the trendy side, you may find Mark is the best option for you. Like Avon, the initial investment to get started is minimal, right at $20.
- **Mary Kay (www.marykay.com):** Also a leader in the direct sales of cosmetics, for over fifty years Mary Kay has offered women the opportunity to start their own business. The initial investment to get started is right at $100.
- **Motives (www.motivescosmetics.marketamerica.com):** Motives is a line of cosmetics that offers professional makeup artists the opportunity to sell directly to their clients and earn up to a 40 percent profit on the products they sell. The annual membership fee is $40, and includes your own branded website to sell product from.

Now that we've explored the world of direct sales cosmetics, let's take a look at another option for supplying product, and that is called private label cosmetics. There is a much greater investment using private label cosmetics than the options we just explored, but for some of you, it might be the right direction, depending on your long-term goals. "Private label" means just that—that you purchase the product from the manufacturer and put your own label on it. The product will be personalized with your name or logo, and you are free to choose the products that best suit the style of makeup your clients need. In fact, if you've ever wondered how someone started their own cosmetic line, it most likely started as private label. Some expenses you'll need to keep in mind if you're considering offering private label products are:

- **Sourcing products:** Many of the private label companies won't have a showroom in your area that you can visit to test the product, so you'll need to order a number of testers and products before you find the products you love. Some companies offer tester packages so you can try a selection of their best-selling products. Most companies will also have websites and catalogs that you can look through before you make a decision.
- **Placing your initial order:** This is a big expense. In order to have a complete line of cosmetics to offer your clients, your initial investment could, and most likely will, run into the thousands. The types of products you choose and the quantity you order of each will dictate your final tally.
- **Minimums:** After you have placed your initial order, you'll need to restock product as you sell it. Be aware that most private label companies will have minimums, meaning you'll need to order a minimum dollar amount of their product each time you place an order.
- **Labels:** Because the products come without labels, you'll want to create a label for each product that will represent your brand. Many of the companies will help you create and print labels for their products for an additional fee, or you can look in your local area for a label maker or print shop to help out. Custom labels can also run into the thousands, especially labels with full-color logos.
- **Insurance:** Another consideration is the product itself and its safety for your client. Reputable labs and manufacturers have already done all the testing necessary for each product, but ask the manufacturer if they offer insurance protection. Many of the companies will add you to their insurance in the event a client has an adverse reaction to something.
- **Website and marketing:** Unlike the direct sales companies, private label companies don't offer any marketing or sales support. If you're interested in selling your private label products online, you'll need to create an online shopping cart and market that site yourself, through your website or other avenues. A simple Google search will produce numerous options for creating and hosting an online shopping cart.

Lady Burd

www.ladyburd.com

Your Name Professional

www.yournamepro.com

Brushes By Karen

www.brushesbykaren.com

Pinnacle Cosmetics (no minimums)

www.pinnaclecosmetics.com

Pure Colors Inc.

www.purecolorsinc.com

Audrey Morris Cosmetics

www.audreymorriscosmetics.com

Color Lab Private Label (custom blending)

www.colorlabprivatelabel.com

Grafton Cosmetics

www.graftoncosmetics.com

Closing Thoughts about the Business

So it's all here—everything I can think of. What has worked for me and what hasn't. Things I've tried and some I haven't. And I know you'll have plenty of ideas of your own. That's what this book is all about: jump-starting your creative juices and getting you on the road to success as a makeup artist.

What I hope the most is that after reading this book from cover to cover, you're inspired to start dreaming. Big things only happen when you dream, and no one can do that for you, except you. Whether you dream about makeup artistry as a part-time way to supplement your income, or as a passion you'd like to pursue full-time, know that the opportunity is out there and waiting for you. All you need to do is get started. And you can get started today. Always remember your business will be as unique as you are. With practice, patience, persistence, and personality, your success as a makeup artist is right around the corner.

Appendix

Schools and Education

The Makeup Designory

New York
375 West Broadway
New York, NY 10012
Phone: (212) 925-9250
www.mud.edu

Los Angeles
129 S. San Fernando Boulevard
Burbank, CA 91502
Phone: (818) 729-9420
www.mud.edu

Europe
Rimska cesta 13, 1000
Ljubljana, Slovenia
Phone: 386 (0) 1 6200 348
www.mud.edu

Cinema Makeup School

3780 Wilshire Boulevard,
Suite 202
Los Angeles, CA 90010
Phone: (213) 368-1234
www.cinemamakeup.com

Joe Blasco Makeup Artist Training Center

Hollywood

1670 Hillhurst Avenue

Hollywood, CA 90027

Phone: (323) 467-4949

www.joeblasco.com

Orlando

5422 Carrier Drive, Suite 304

Orlando, FL 32819

Phone: (407) 363-1234

www.joeblasco.com

Cosmix School of Makeup Artistry

2635 East Oakland Park Boulevard

Fort Lauderdale, FL 33306

Toll-Free: (800) 908-0544

Phone: (954) 564-4181

www.cosmixinc.com

CAMMUA—Couture Academy of Modern Makeup Artistry

4500 Campus Drive,

Suite 650

Newport Beach, CA 92660

Phone: (949) 798-0010

www.cammua.com

Academy of Freelance Makeup, New York

318 W. 39th Street

New York, NY 10018

Phone: (212) 710-1334

www.aofmakeup.com

Boca Beauty Academy

7820 Glades Road

Boca Raton, FL 33434

Phone: (561) 487-1191

www.bocabeauty.com

Vancouver Film School

200–198 W. Hastings Street

Vancouver, British Columbia

Canada V6B 1H2

Phone: (800) 661-4101

www.vfs.com/makeupdesign

EI School of Professional Makeup

1622 N. Highland Avenue

Hollywood, CA 90028

Phone: (323) 871-8318

www.ei.edu

Online Resource and Industry Magazine

Makeup Artist Magazine is an internationally read publication and online resource that is dedicated to the craft of makeup artistry, featuring articles on the entertainment industry's top makeup artists, the most innovative makeup techniques, current product news, and other information pertaining to the makeup industry. Subscriptions are available.

The online website www.makeupmag.com provides information on trade shows, schools, and education, a library of makeup-related books for purchase, and other industry news.

Recommended Reading

By Author

Bobbi Brown

Bobbi Brown has become an iconic makeup artist and the voice of the everyday woman. You can purchase her books at www.bobbibrowncosmetics.com.

Bobbi Brown Beauty Rules: Fabulous Looks, Beauty Essentials, and Life Lessons. Chronicle Books, 2010.

Bobbi Brown's sixth book, *Beauty Rules,* is a fresh, energetic beauty bible for young women. Bobbi Brown's goal is to help women "look and feel like themselves, only prettier and more confident." And true to this philosophy, *Beauty Rules* was written to help young women learn the beauty basics and then ultimately find their own style.

Bobbi Brown Makeup Manual: For Everyone from Beginner to Pro, reprint edition. Grand Central Life & Style, 2011.

Bobbi's twenty-five-plus years of makeup artist experience is distilled into one volume that includes full-color photos and step-by-step instructions, as well as a "Ten-Step Guide to Perfect Makeup" that teaches you how to apply your makeup in ten minutes or less. Packed with all the tricks of the trade, this book also offers a unique guide for aspiring makeup artists: how to break into the business, put together a portfolio, book work, and work with photographers, magazine editors, fashion designers, and celebrities.

Bobbi Brown Living Beauty, reprint edition. Springboard Press, 2009.

Bobbi Brown has written this book for women over forty. Bobbi shows how skin care and makeup can instantly make you look fresher and better. With step-by-step makeup instructions, nutrition and fitness tips, and inspiring quotes from celebrities and countless beautiful women, this book is a celebration of beauty at any age.

Bobbi Brown Beauty: The Ultimate Beauty Resource. Collins Living, 1998.

Bobbi has taken all of her beauty knowledge, experience, and philosophy and incorporated it into a beauty guide for women of all ages. The book addresses important beauty concerns about tools, makeup elements, bad beauty days, how to wear foundation, beauty during pregnancy, and skin care, as well as easy-to-follow makeup routines.

Bobbi Brown Beauty Evolution: A Guide to a Lifetime of Beauty. No publisher listed.

This book is a celebration of beauty across the generations. It was written to help women feel good about themselves at any age. This important guide covers it all, with Bobbi devoting chapters on beauty from the age of twenty to seventy and beyond, discussing issues that matter most to women, and sharing the lessons she herself has learned from her own personal evolution.

Bobbi Brown Teenage Beauty: Everything You Need to Look Pretty, Natural, Sexy and Awesome. William Morrow Paperbacks, 2001.

Bobbi Brown writes a hip, fresh, no-nonsense beauty bible specifically for teens, offering basic skin care and makeup tips and techniques to last a lifetime.

Kevyn Aucoin

Celebrity makeup artist and a true master of his craft, Kevyn's books are both instructional and inspirational. He was truly a revered makeup artist, and his artistry still shines through in his books.

Face Forward. Little, Brown and Company, 2001.

Conceived as an exploration of the past, present, and future of beauty, *Face Forward* is a showcase of the transformative, creative possibilities of makeup, with portraits of everyone from Julia Roberts to Sharon Stone, Martha Stewart to Kevyn's mother, Thelma. Throughout, Aucoin offers step-by-step instruction, personal commentary on each look and model, and his feelings on topics such as friendship, politics, and the environment.

Making Faces. Little, Brown and Company, 1999.

The first section offers Kevyn's favorite ideas, tricks, and techniques for enhancing, defining, and altering facial features with makeup. You'll learn how to care for your skin, what foundation to use with your skin type, and transformational magic for that central player in the drama of beauty: eyes. The book contains transformative before and afters and dozens of different looks.

The Art of Makeup. Perennial Currents, 1996.

The Art of Makeup is a collection of star-studded portraits, and Kevyn offers some of the techniques that helped earn him his superstar status in the fashion industry. It also features tips to help women achieve the Aucoin look. Through step-by-step instructions, sample makeovers, and an explanation of the ten most common beauty mistakes and the four basic makeup combinations, Aucoin helps women accentuate their positive features, enhance their beauty, and look and feel their best.

Sam Fine

Celebrity makeup artist and beauty expert, Sam Fine has created and refined techniques that enhance the beauty of women of color. *Vogue* has called him the "go-to makeup master for women of color." His book and instructional DVD can be purchased at www.amazon.com.

Fine Beauty, reprint edition. Riverhead Trade, 1999.

Makeup artist to African-American models and other black stars, Fine shares his beauty secrets here, offering tips on all the fundamentals of applying makeup with clear, step-by-step instructions.

Fine: The Basics of Beauty. Directed by Paul Starkman. Cergol Films, 2009.

This step-by-step DVD tutorial is a follow-up to his book and features three individual makeovers and addresses myriad beauty challenges by focusing on tools, techniques, and product selection. Sharing his wealth of experience and expertise, Fine enables viewers to fully understand all of the intricacies that go into creating a flawless face.

Taylor Chang-Babaian

A celebrity makeup expert shares her secrets in the first beauty guide for all Asian women.

Asian Faces: The Essential Beauty and Makeup Guide for Asian Women. Perigee Trade, 2007.

Asian Faces is the first beauty book created specifically to focus on the techniques and styles that enhance the skin tones and facial features of Asian women of all ages and ethnicities. The book is fully illustrated and offers step-by-step instructions.

Style Eyes. Perigee Trade, 2010.

In *Style Eyes,* Taylor shares her highly sought-after beauty tips and techniques that will help you create the perfect eye look for any occasion. Included are step-by-step techniques for every eye shape and every occasion.

Jemma Kidd

An internationally recognized makeup artist and founder of a popular makeup school in London, Jemma Kidd also has a line of makeup sold exclusively in over 1,600 Target stores.

"Millions of women throughout the world wear makeup, but few of them have been taught how to apply it." This is what inspired leading international makeup artist Jemma Kidd's vision for her makeup school, product line, and now her book, which aims to teach a new generation of women how to use the latest and best techniques.

Jemma Kidd Make-up Masterclass: Beauty Bible of Professional Techniques and Wearable Looks. St. Martin's Press, 2009.

This book demystifies the art of makeup and shows women how to enhance their best features and feel confident in their appearance, whatever their age or lifestyle. It includes insider secrets, and practical step-by-step instructions and techniques that maximize beauty. Jemma also illustrates how extreme looks can be adapted and toned down for everyday wear.

Francois Nars
Francois Nars is the creator of NARS cosmetics and one of the master makeup artists of our time.

Makeup Your Mind: Express Yourself. Rizzoli, 2001.

In this book, Nars combines his expertise in makeup and photography to create this makeover manual, and then illustrates how makeup can become the ultimate form of self-expression. This definitive do-it-yourself guide is perfect for any aspiring artist interested in the transformative power of cosmetics.

Historical Reading
Fashions in Makeup: From Ancient to Modern Times, 3rd edition, by Richard Corson. Peter Owen Ltd., 2004.

An encyclopedic book that takes you through the history of makeup, from ancient Egypt to the present. Richard Corson taught theatrical makeup in colleges and universities throughout the United States and worked as a theatrical makeup consultant. This book and his other fashion-based historical reference books are available at www.amazon.com.

Retro Makeup Styling
These books walk you through vintage makeup looks and techniques. They are all available at www.amazon.com.

Makeup: 1930s Beauty Instruction and Technique by Virginia Vincent. Bramcost Publications, 2008.

This rare makeup and beauty book contains detailed instructions and illustrations for makeup application as worn by women of the early 1930s. The book was originally printed in 1932, and not only gives you authentic techniques but also walks you through the color choices that were in vogue at the time.

Beauty, Glamour & Personality—A Complete 1940s Guide to Vintage Makeup, Hairstyling and Elegance by Ern Westmore and Bud Westmore. Bramcost Publications, 2011.

This book was originally published in 1947 and contains all of the information needed to create the starlet looks of the 1940s. This book walks you through the beauty and corrective techniques used by professional makeup artists on the film sirens of the day.

Westmore Beauty Book—A Complete 1950s Guide to Vintage Makeup, Hairstyling and Beauty Techniques by Bud Westmore, Perc Westmore, Frank Westmore, and Mont Westmore. Bramcost Publications, 2009.

Originally published in 1956, this makeup, beauty, and hairstyling book contains all of the information needed to create the glamorous movie-star look of the 1950s. The book will show you how to analyze, transform, and perfect yourself into a 1950s vision.

Trade Shows

International Make-Up Artist Trade Show
www.imats.net

The International Make-Up Artist Trade Show is the makeup world's biggest gathering of makeup artists, vendors, and makeup enthusiasts. Makeup pros from fashion and media provide educational seminars and demonstrations. You can also view the newest products on the market.

The show is held six times annually—in London in January; New York in April; Los Angeles in June; Vancouver, B.C., in July; Sydney in September; and Toronto in November.

The Makeup Show
www.themakeupshow.com

The Makeup Show is an industry event for pros, bringing the best and brightest in the industry together for hands-on seminars, keynote speakers, and exhibitors, all demonstrating the newest products on the market.

The Makeup Show is held annually in Los Angeles, New York City, Chicago, and Europe.

Index

About the Author

Photo courtesy of Steve Depino, www.stevedepino.com

d.d. Nickel has been working in the beauty industry as a professional makeup artist, educator, and beauty expert for over fifteen years. Her real interest in makeup began after a chance meeting with a renowned makeup artist shortly after her move to New York City. She spent the early years of her career assisting him on celebrity and industry shoots, and was instrumental in growing his retail business as national makeup artist and director of education. In the latter position, d.d. conceptualized and wrote the educational materials used in training makeup artists across the country in stores like Barneys New York, Nordstrom, and Sephora.

She has spent the last dozen years as a successful freelance makeup artist, working on popular television shows, commercials, print, Broadway, red carpets, New York Fashion Week, and with countless celebrities. One of her first freelance opportunities was with E! Entertainment, where she spent several seasons working on the hit TLC show, *What Not to Wear*. She created the look for the Tony Award–winning lead of the Broadway show, *Wonderful Town*, and has helped countless celebrities look their best on screen and on red carpets from Cannes to Los Angeles. In addition to launching a successful freelance career, she also continued to write and create training materials for Victoria's Secret Beauty, used in stores across the country.

In 2006, d.d. opened a makeup studio near her home in New Haven, Connecticut, offering private lessons and her signature line of makeup, d.d.Nickel, now available online at www.ddnickel.com. In early 2007, she began offering on-location services for the bride and bridal party. Her studio and bridal beauty business has more than doubled each year and continues to grow.